Systematic Synthesis of Qualitative Research

POCKET GUIDES TO
SOCIAL WORK RESEARCH METHODS

Series Editor
Tony Tripodi, DSW
Professor Emeritus, Ohio State University

MICHAEL SAINI
ARON SHLONSKY

Systematic Synthesis
of Qualitative Research

OXFORD
UNIVERSITY PRESS

Oxford University Press, Inc., publishes works that further
Oxford University's objective of excellence
in research, scholarship, and education.

Oxford   New York
Auckland   Cape Town   Dar es Salaam   Hong Kong   Karachi
Kuala Lumpur   Madrid   Melbourne   Mexico City   Nairobi
New Delhi   Shanghai   Taipei   Toronto

With offices in
Argentina   Austria   Brazil   Chile   Czech Republic   France   Greece
Guatemala   Hungary   Italy   Japan   Poland   Portugal   Singapore
South Korea   Switzerland   Thailand   Turkey   Ukraine   Vietnam

Published in the United States of America by Oxford University Press, Inc.
198 Madison Avenue, New York, New York 10016
www.oup.com

Oxford is a registered trade mark of Oxford University Press
in the UK and in certain other countries
© 2012 Oxford University Press, Inc.

Library of Congress Cataloging-in-Publication Data

Saini, Michael.
Systematic synthesis of qualitative research / Michael Saini, Aron Shlonsky.
p. cm. — (Pocket guides to social work research methods)
Includes bibliographical references and index.
ISBN 978-0-19-538721-6   1. Social service—Research—
Methodology.   2. Qualitative research—Methodology.   I. Shlonsky, Aron.   II. Title.
HV11.S266 2012
001.4'2—dc23
2011036240

Typeset in Minion
Printed on acid-free paper
Printed in the United States of America

Contents

Preface

"What works in child welfare" (Kluger, Alexander, & Curtis, 2000). "What works for troubled children," (Buchanan & Ritchie, 2004). "What works for parents with learning disabilities" (McGaw, 2000). These titles reflect an interest in what is effective in social work policy and practice and are part of a growing body of literature aimed at improving outcomes for clients receiving services from social workers and others in the helping professions and understanding the systems that impede or facilitate the delivery of these services.

Notwithstanding this expressed interest in harnessing evidence for effective social work practice and policy and a simultaneous, parallel growth of quantitative and qualitative evidence relevant to social work, there remains a lack of attention paid to building a cumulative body of evidence to inform social work practice and policy. This means that it is difficult to identify gaps in knowledge so that new research questions can be asked that are relevant to the experiences of populations served by social work. For clinicians, the challenge of including the best available evidence within practice decisions with clients is overwhelming given the ever-increasing volume of studies on specific areas of social work practice. Social workers often have little time and insufficient resources to adequately make sense of the best available evidence needed to guide practice. Literature reviews can only go so far and are notoriously biased. Without systematic summaries of individual studies, the task of making sense of the evidence, both within and across studies, is a daunting endeavor.

Systematic reviews are designed to deal with this very problem and are an integral part of evidence-based practice. They can be thought of as an overarching approach for the review of evidence and are generally understood to include a set of preformulated questions, comprehensive methods for searching and locating primary studies, a transparent method for appraising quality, and explicit procedures for synthesizing included studies. Although not typically included in the discourse of systematic reviews and evidence-based practice, knowledge gained from qualitative research can not only describe elements of interventions that "work," but can also be helpful in answering questions about why interventions work (or do not work) and the influence these interventions may have (or do not have) on clients that the interventions are meant to target. As important as "Did it work?" type of questions, qualitative studies might ask: How do people experience the intervention? Why might an intervention work, for whom, and in what circumstances? What aspects of the intervention are valued and why is this so? What system level factors contribute to the successful implementation of an intervention? What conditions create potential barriers for recruitment and participation in an intervention? Within the context of evidence-based practice, qualitative research can also be the primary source of data to answer questions that do not focus solely on social services' efficacy or effectiveness (Gough & Elbourne, 2002) but, instead, focus on the richly described perceptions of clients and the contextual considerations that influence the delivery of services including: the perceived needs of clients; clients' experiences of services; the presence of program champions or leaders; the operation and resources for services; the cultural appropriateness, relevance, and sensitivity of services; aspects related to training; and the presence or absence of collaboration among partners in supporting the services.

Arguments are often made about the contingent nature of evidence gleaned from synthesis of qualitative studies and the current lack of consensus about the veracity of some of its aspects. And yet, despite these hesitations, qualitative synthesis can be included within the family of systematic reviews as a unique method for answering research questions, as well a method that compliments and enhances other systematic review methods. Systematic synthesis is an important technique and, used suitably, can deepen our understanding of the contextual dimensions of social work practice, and can help to move qualitative synthesis out of the shadow of quantitative synthesis (i.e., meta-analysis). Moreover, qualitative synthesis provides impetus to the creation of methods that are transparent, consistent, and rigorous, regardless of the systematic review method, and helps to distinguish qualitative synthesis from other types of reviews of the literature.

PURPOSE OF THE BOOK

This book aims to provide graduate students, social work researchers, and practitioners with current standards, philosophical debates, and methods for understanding and conducting systematic qualitative synthesis. An overview of the range of qualitative synthesis methods available is provided so that readers may choose a method that is most consistent with the important questions they are asking, which will, ultimately, better inform practice and policy decisions relevant to social work. In doing so, we also introduce and explain the terminology found within this emerging field of research to provide a clear roadmap for those inclined to pursue this challenging, yet rewarding method of inquiry.

Like others who have considered these issues (Dixon-Woods, Bonas, Booth, et al., 2006; Paterson, Thorne, Canam, & Jillings, 2001; Pope, Mays, & Popay, 2007; Sandelowski & Barroso, 2007), we are not naïve to the challenges involved in articulating systematic methods for synthesizing qualitative studies. We acknowledge the risk that presenting an approach for qualitative synthesis poses. We may overemphasize methods over substance and readers might perceive that we are prescribing a single method. Moreover, the philosophical differences between, say, a post-positivist grounded theory study and a critical–realist ethnographic study cannot be ignored. Both are qualitative studies, yet how can they be compared? Indeed, this is what makes a quantitative systematic review much easier because there is just one philosophical tradition to contend with: post-positivism. Quantitative meta-reviews compare findings generated by different designs and statistical techniques, but, for the most part, each study enacts the same basic post-positivist assumptions (e.g., that differences between people can be observed, aggregated, interpreted, and generalized).

We acknowledge that our epistemological and ontological frameworks may further challenge us in preserving the integrity and enhancing the utility of qualitative research within multiple perspectives. Specifically, we understand that methods for synthesis are theory-laden and inherently biased by cultural experiences and worldviews. That is, the author of such studies cannot remove herself from the context in which she sits. Nonetheless, we believe that some shared meanings can emerge from multiple studies even though these meanings can change over time and must always remain connected to the context of the original studies (frankly, we believe this is true of quantitative studies as well!). This book will not resolve the debates. As advocates for the inclusion of qualitative studies in evidence-based practice and data synthesis, we will focus on the research questions at hand to choose the best fit of methods. Within this view, qualitative synthesis is an opportunity to enhance the "utilization value" (Smaling, 2003, p. 60) and "power" (Kearney, 1998b) of qualitative research (Sandelowski & Barroso, 2007).

Based on our experiences of using the best available evidence to answer different research questions, we propose a systematic synthesis approach to enhance transparency, consistency, and rigor while still responding to the central philosophical challenges of including qualitative studies. Careful attention is made to present an approach whereby studies are grouped with similar epistemological and ontological frameworks to promote philosophical consistency throughout the synthesis process. The approach is presented with enough information about the controversies to allow readers an opportunity to form their own opinion and to provide the information they need to avoid some of the major philosophical and methodological pitfalls they will surely encounter.

This book presents an approach for planning, developing, and implementing qualitative synthesis within existing protocols and guidelines. The book also covers a number of the methodological challenges inherent in such an approach, including: the philosophical tensions of including qualitative synthesis within the broader family of systematic reviews; the balance of comprehensive and iterative information retrieval strategies to locate and screen qualitative research; the use of appraisal tools to assess the quality of qualitative studies; the various approaches to synthesize qualitative studies, including interpretive, integrated, and aggregative; and the tensions between the generalizability and transferability of findings that emerge from qualitative synthesis.

The content and format of the book reflect the authors' experience in conducting systematic reviews and primary qualitative research within evidence-based practice. The book includes examples relevant to social work to illustrate these approaches and explores the benefits, limitations, and pitfalls of qualitative synthesis within existing systematic review protocols. The book will hopefully inspire others to consider questions relevant to social work to help build our collective understanding of the various ways that qualitative synthesis can help inform practice, research, and policy decisions.

OUTLINE OF THE BOOK

The book is divided into three parts. The first part looks at the evolution of qualitative research within the framework of evidence-based practice and its inclusion in the family of systematic reviews. This part briefly recounts the history of qualitative systematic reviews across disciplines and within systematic review enterprises, including the Cochrane and the Campbell Collaborations. We argue for a nonhierarchical approach to systematic reviews, where each method within the broad family of systematic reviews (e.g., meta-analysis, qualitative synthesis, rapid evidence assessments) is understood to have a complimentary, unique approach based on the type of question being asked and the needs of the stakeholders. In this section, current methods for conducting qualitative syntheses are explored by presenting various models of aggregation, integration, and interpretation of qualitative findings across studies. The common link among these different models is that they all attempt to draw out findings across qualitative studies to generate new insights and understandings (McDermott, Graham, & Hamilton, 2004). Within the presentation of these models, we draw out the epistemological frameworks and underlying assumptions of each of these models to provide the reader with some direction for choosing methods for specific types of questions and purposes. We also explore the integration of qualitative research within quantitative systematic reviews.

Part II provides an approach for conducting systematic syntheses of qualitative research within the family of systematic reviews by offering suggestions for developing information-retrieval strategies for qualitative synthesis consistent with current guidelines produced by both the Cochrane and Campbell Collaborations. Strategies for using qualitative research as the primary source of studies included in a systematic review are also explored. Once primary studies are included within the systematic review process, researchers often struggle to appraise the evidence. While acknowledging the long-standing debate regarding the appraisal of qualitative studies, we introduce a study appraisal form that has been created to assess methodological rigor, credibility, dependability, confirmability, transferability, and relevance within and across qualitative studies; and we provide an illustration regarding the applicability of the appraisal form. To illustrate the inclusion of qualitative studies within the family of systematic reviews, we present a working systematic review that includes both intervention studies and qualitative studies to assess family group decision making within the context of child protection services.

Part III discusses using qualitative evidence to create actionable knowledge and the application of the products of qualitative synthesis in practice. We also provide suggestions for a more seamless integration of qualitative reviews within both the evidence-based practice movement and other systematic review methods.

The overall framework for synthesizing qualitative research presented in this book is intended to develop methods that are rigorous, relevant, transparent, systematic, and applicable to a broad audience of researchers, policy makers, decision makers, social work students, and social work practitioners. Although the process of conducting a synthesis of qualitative research is presented in a cumulative format, each chapter is independently organized to allow readers to use this text both as a source book for conducting a systematic synthesis and as a pocket guide for the inclusion of qualitative studies and appraisal geared toward increasing the rigor, credibility, applicability, and transferability of primary qualitative studies.

Acknowledgments

We are grateful for the ground-breaking work of other authors who have gone before us, particularly, Julie Barroso, Andrew Booth, Mary Dixon-Woods, Angela Harden, Karin Hannes, Nicholas Mays, Alan Pearson, Jennie Popay, Catherine Pope, and Margaret Sandelowski. These trailblazers have been instrumental in developing the roadmap for the inclusion of qualitative research within systematic reviews and shedding light on both the rewards and challenges of synthesizing qualitative studies. This book would not have been possible without their detailed attention and analysis to the considerations and cautions of integrating interpretive data across studies. We also want to acknowledge the many methodologists, policy makers, and practitioners who participated in our workshops at the Cochrane and Campbell Collaboration Colloquiums in Canada, Norway, England, and the Unites States and at the First European Social Work Research Conference in Oxford in 2011.

We express our deepest gratitude to Carmen Logie for her research assistance for this project by assisting in reviewing the various qualitative synthesis methods. We are significantly indebted to Rory Crath for his tremendous contributions and prodigious editorial support, as well as for sharing his profound insight in mapping the philosophical terrain needed to present this project in a coherent, logical, and concise fashion. Rory was instrumental in helping to shape our approach for including qualitative synthesis within systematic reviews. Rory has expertise in investigating the imperatives of the aesthetic in social work practice, the workings of globalization and neo-liberal rationalities and technologies, and theories of justice and equity. This contextual understanding of the role of qualitative studies within diverse populations has substantially contributed to a more sophisticated presentation of this important work for social work practice, research, and policy.

This project could not have been possible without the tremendous support and guidance of Maura Roessner, Senior Editor for Oxford University Press, Inc. We are appreciative to Maura for her unwavering support and solicitous encouragement throughout the project and for helping us move this manuscript along to completion.

Systematic Synthesis of Qualitative Research

Part I

The Integration of Qualitative Research within Evidence-Based Practice

1

Evolution of Qualitative Synthesis within Systematic Reviews

Far better an approximate answer to the right question, which is often vague, than an exact answer to the wrong question, which can always be made precise

—(John Tukey, 1962, p. 13)

SYSTEMATIC REVIEWS TO GUIDE SOCIAL WORK PRACTICE AND POLICY

The process of evidence-based practice (EBP) is currently understood as the intersection of current best evidence, client state and circumstances, and client values and expectations (Sackett, Richardson, Rosenberg, & Haynes, 1997). The optimal integration of these three areas can be seen as clinical expertise (Haynes, Devereaux, & Guyatt, 2002). Although such an overarching approach is appealing on a number of different levels, not the least of which is the anticipated benefits to clients, social services have struggled to create a body of research sufficiently large and of valid methodology to revolutionize practice. Ensuring the implementation of evidence-based practice in social work requires an ongoing commitment from researchers, policy makers, and social work practitioners to use systematic and rigorous methods for obtaining and using evidence in practice. The critical question concerning EBP is not whether evidence should play a role in clinical decisions, but how to efficiently and effectively establish this role (Haynes, Sackett, Gray, Cook, & Guyatt, 1996).

Systematic reviews are an essential component of EBP. Indeed, they are the primary vehicle for preparing, maintaining, and disseminating high-quality and relevant evidence to be used in practice. According to Littell and Corcoran (2010), systematic reviews are "carefully organized, comprehensive, and transparent studies of previous research on a particular topic. Systematic reviews follow written protocols (detailed plans) that specify the central objectives, concepts, and methods in advance" (p. 313). These methodologically prescribed and highly structured syntheses of the literature are conducted to address a particular question (or set of questions) that arise in the practice or policy environments (Petticrew & Roberts, 2006) and can be thought of as an effective means of comprehending how the results from a single study fit within, and enhance previous research on, a similar issue (Mulrow, 1994). Most importantly, systematic reviews attempt to decrease the bias of traditional literature reviews by systematically and transparently synthesizing the greatest range of relevant, high-quality studies, published and unpublished, related to a single, prespecified question.

There are now a number of guidelines for conducting systematic reviews (see Littell, Corcoran, & Pillai, 2008; Petticrew & Roberts, 2006). These guidelines include procedures for identifying the literature to be included, steps for critically appraising the evidence, methods for synthesizing the results, and frameworks for presenting the results of previous studies (Littell & Corcoran, 2010). In contrast, traditional reviews (Littell, Corcoran, & Pillai, 2008) tend to arrange studies according to an already rehearsed argument, and such reviews often amount to a discussion of the literature known to the author, complete with opinions and conjecture. Even though such approaches may make for good and, at times, useful reading, they also open the door for substantial bias due to a lack of transparency and clear criteria for choosing which studies to include and elaborate on. There is evidence that such bias exists. For instance, there is substantial evidence for publishing bias (i.e., studies with significant findings tend to be published more often than studies with null findings) (Petticrew & Roberts, 2006), as well as selective reporting of outcome data (i.e., only certain findings from studies are included in traditional literature reviews, and these tend to favor positive findings of interventions) (Chan, Hróbjartsson, Haarh, Gøzsche, & Altman, 2004). Systematic reviews address questions left dangling by traditional forms of review: Why were particular studies chosen? What makes one study more important than another? Would another author with the same question come up with a different set of conclusions? What are the strengths and quality each study brings to the overall review? What are the types of measures used to reach conclusions and (if a meta-analysis was conducted) what are the overall effect sizes for various constructs across studies (Gough & Elbourne, 2002)?

The Cochrane Collaboration and the Campbell Collaboration are two international, interdisciplinary research networks that are dedicated to helping health and social care professionals make well-informed practice and policy decisions by preparing, maintaining, and disseminating systematic reviews. The Cochrane Collaboration boasts over than ten thousand volunteers in more than 90 countries who review the effects of health care interventions using state-of-the-art systematic review methods, and these are published in the Cochrane Library (http://www2.cochrane.org/reviews/). The Campbell Collaboration focuses on the preparation of systematic reviews in the general fields of social welfare, education, crime and justice, and international development, these are published in the Campbell Library (www.campbellcollaboration.org/library). Both collaborations apply rigorous and systematic procedures to review the effects of interventions, with the aim of establishing a world library of systematic reviews that are made widely available to interested stakeholders. Systematic reviews can also be published in journals, books, or on government websites, though such reviews may not adhere to the high standards of these two collaborations.

To date, systematic reviews have been mostly focused on examining the efficacy and effectiveness of specific interventions, when possible using meta-analysis, which is "a set of statistical methods for combining quantitative results from multiple studies to produce an overall summary of empirical knowledge on a given topic" (Littell, et al., 2008, p. 299). Randomized controlled trials (RCTs) and other highly controlled studies are required for examining the efficacy or effectiveness of an intervention because such designs have fewer threats to internal validity, thus providing the best evidence of a causal relationship between an intervention and an outcome (Pettricrew & Roberts, 2006).

Unfortunately, many have taken evidence-based practice to mean that practice and policy should be based solely on the evidence produced by RCTs. As Ramchandani, Joughin, and Zwi (2001) suggest, "this narrow approach, whilst not one envisaged by the original proponents of evidence-based medicine...., is a common misunderstanding of the paradigm" (p. 60). Although RCTs have been considered the "gold standard" for questions of effectiveness, Lewis notes there are serious gaps in indiscriminately applying RCTs to answer evidence-based questions, as many research questions are not amenable to research designs involving RCTs (Lewis 1998). If the basic steps of EBP involve posing client-oriented, answerable questions, appraising what is found, and integrating current best evidence with client preference/values and clinical state/circumstances (as outlined in Sackett et al., 1997), then surely the wealth of information derived from qualitative studies, especially as it relates to client context, is both relevant and important.

THE EMERGENCE OF QUALITATIVE SYNTHESIS

Qualitative methodology is fast becoming the approach of choice for many social work investigators who are seeking answers to intriguing research questions, pushing the field to question long-held beliefs, or simply exploring what is occurring in the world of clients, practitioners, students, and related groups. The integration of qualitative data to inform policy and practice directions is already underway in areas such as homelessness (Meadows-Oliver, 2006); sexual violence (Draucker et al., 2009), health, and well-being (Harvey, 2007); injection drug use (Treloar & Rhodes, 2009); eating disorders (Espíndola & Blay, 2009); and parenting programs (Kane, Wood, & Barlow, 2007). Yet how are we to know which qualitative studies have results we can count on? Or, what do we do when two studies have opposite findings? And how do we synthesize or weave together findings from a number of studies in the same topic area with the least amount of bias?

As currently understood, qualitative synthesis is a method that attempts to address these questions pertaining to how qualitative studies are aggregated, integrated, and/or interpreted (Sandelowski & Barroso, 2007). Similar to other systematic review methods (e.g., meta-analysis), researchers conducting syntheses of qualitative studies have an interest in using a transparent, consistent, and comprehensive process to integrate findings from empirical studies and to generate new conceptualization of the target phenomenon (Meeker & Jezewski, 2008). Synthesizing qualitative research is unique, however, because part of the process of assessing the feasibility of combining findings across studies involves consideration of the various worldviews and paradigms underlying each primary study. Therefore, such syntheses must not only combine similar studies but must include processes that allow the research to "remain faithful to the interpretive rendering in each particular study" (Sandelowski & Barroso, 2003b, p. 154).

Qualitative approaches have traditionally been excluded from systematic reviews due in part to challenges confronting researchers when they attempt to synthesize studies with the diverse range of methodologies and epistemologies employed in the qualitative research field (These considerations are further explored at the end of the chapter). The tides are slowly turning, however. There is a growing list of texts and articles devoted to improving the methods for including qualitative reviews within the family of systematic reviews (e.g., see Dixon-Woods, Agarwal, Jones, Young, & Sutton, 2005; Harden & Thomas, 2005; Petticrew & Roberts, 2006; Pope, Mays & Popay, 2007; Sandelowski & Barroso, 2007). Moreover, there are now numerous approaches for conducting qualitative synthesis. Methods have been developed specifically for including qualitative primary studies, whereas other methods have been created to combine quantitative and qualitative studies. When qualitative reviews compliment quantitative reviews, the qualitative component has the unique role of helping to define and refine the question (thus allowing for maximum relevance) and to synthesize descriptive evidence about interventions that bear on findings of effectiveness (Popay, 2006).

Important to this trajectory has been the identification by international organizations, including the Cochrane and Campbell Collaborations, of the need to develop methods for integrating qualitative studies within conventional systematic reviews (Higgins & Green, 2008). Although no current template is in place to guide the inclusion of qualitative studies within Cochrane Collaboration reviews, there are now examples that have nested qualitative reviews within systematic reviews of effectiveness (see Ryan et al., 2011). In the context of a quantitative systematic review, a synthesis of qualitative studies in the relevant field should be considered if it will: (a) contribute to the development of a more robust intervention by helping to define an intervention more precisely; (b) assist in the choice of outcome measures and assist in the development of valid research questions; and (c) help to understand heterogeneous results from studies of effect (Campbell Collaboration). Based on these guidelines, a review that contains descriptions of qualitative research relevant to the topic of interest should operationally describe the: (a) criteria for inclusion and exclusion of studies, (b) methods used in primary research, (c) criteria for determining independent findings, and (d) characteristics of included studies. Though not yet formally accepted, these guidelines indicate that a qualitative synthesis can augment a Campbell Collaboration review by providing not only in-depth understandings of the experiences and perceptions of people involved in interventions, but can be used to bring forth meaningful explorations of important issues related to implementation of an intervention as well. Finally, qualitative synthesis is proposed as a method for potentially adding evidence to the generation or refutation of hypotheses, contributing to the development of a more robust intervention by helping to define an intervention more precisely, assisting in the choice of outcome measures and the development of valid research questions, and helping to explain heterogeneous results from studies of efficacy and effectiveness.

Although these initiatives have made significant strides toward the inclusion of qualitative studies, there remain no clear guidelines for those wanting to include only qualitative primary studies within a Campbell Collaboration systematic review and qualitative syntheses will not be accepted as Campbell reviews, on their own, until such a time as these standards are developed and accepted. The inclusion of qualitative synthesis methods in systematic reviews of effectiveness generally fall within an enhancement model (Popay, Arai, & Roen, 2003), where qualitative methods are seen to complement or augment the relevance of quantitative findings. Dixon-Woods, Bonas, et al., (2006) propose that qualitative synthesis methods can also fall within a "difference model" (p. 32), where qualitative methods are developed independently to contribute to a different kind of evidence relevant for practice and policy. Social workers and decision makers require not only "what works" in terms of interventions, but also "what is at work" in regards to the integration of clients' perspectives, professional wisdom, and contextual factors within various systems relevant to practice and policy.

We propose that some topics are best addressed solely with qualitative studies due to the nature of the question posed, the purpose of the review, the extent to which sources of high-quality quantitative data are available, and the very real barriers to conducting rigorous quantitative studies for particular types of questions and types of designs articulated to shed light on a relatively unexplored topic area or a difficult to reach population.

WHAT WE MEAN BY "QUALITATIVE RESEARCH"

Qualitative research is best referred to as a complex family of research methods (Denzin & Lincoln, 1994), with numerous investigators now exploring the various methods and designs appropriate for addressing questions germane to social work research (e.g., see Gilgun, 2009; Riessman, 1993; Padgett, 2008; Shaw & Gould, 2001; Sherman & Reid, 1994). As these investigators suggest, there is no "one size fits all" (Padgett, 1998, p. 1) and some members of the family of qualitative research are more compatible than others (Denzin & Lincoln, 1994). Various writers have weighed in on attempting to identify the markers of what is uniquely constitutive of qualitative research. Denzin and Lincoln (2000), for example, suggest that qualitative research is a situated activity that locates the observer in the world and consists of a set of interpretive, material practices that make that world visible. For these investigators, research is multimethod in focus and involves the studied use and collection of a variety of empirical materials—"case study, personal experience, intro-spective, life story, interview, observational, historical, interactional, and visual texts that describe routine and problematic moments and mean-ings in individuals' lives" (p. 2). Creswell (1998) emphasizes the rele-vance of qualitative inquiry for building "a complex, holistic picture" and reporting "detailed views of informants" (p. 15). Other investigators stress the importance of qualitative research for drawing out the mean-ing of particular activities or beliefs within naturalistic and contextual-ized systems (Padgett, 1998) or in the context of the culture being considered (Valadez & Bamberger, 1994).

For the purposes of this book, we find it useful to consider Royse, Thyer, Padgett, and Logan's (2006) helpful summary when thinking about the complexity of the qualitative research family: "virtually all qualitative studies, regardless of their epistemological backdrop, share in common a few key ingredients: 1) a focus on naturalistic inquiry in situation;

2) a reliance on the researcher as the instrument of data collection; and 3) reports emphasising narrative over numbers" (p. 88). This qualitative framework that we adopt in this book does, however, limit the types of qualitative studies that may be included in what we mean by qualitative research. In doing so, we acknowledge that we may overemphasize the kinds of qualitative research that produce findings derived from "real-world settings" (Golafshani, 2003, p. 600), in which "phenomenon of interest unfolds naturally" (Patton, 2001, p. 39). Our focus is purposive because naturalistic inquiry is most germane for qualitative synthesis given the ontological and epistemological consistencies of connecting knowledge that is understood to emerge from these naturalistic research settings to inform us about what we might do in real-life circumstances with real-life clients. (see Box 1.1).

DISTINCTION OF QUALITATIVE AND QUANTITATIVE RESEARCH

In comparing qualitative research to quantitative methods, Padgett (1998) states that both approaches are empirical, systematic, and based on scientific inquiry. However, qualitative researchers are more likely to follow an inductive approach (e.g., to derive concepts from the social reality of the respondents) compared with the deductive methods prescribed by quantitative designs (e.g., to apply social science theory to the social reality). Table 1.1 summarizes (and overstates) some of the differences between qualitative and quantitative research. However, in reality, there is a great deal of overlap between them, and the importance of the commonalities is increasingly being recognized (Abell, 1990; Greenhalgh & Taylor, 1997). For instance, Padgett claims that "contrary to a popular misconception, qualitative research is neither haphazard nor unfocused. Yet systematic research need not be prescriptive and rigidly predictable. It can also be flexible" (p. 4).

REASONS FOR INCLUDING QUALITATIVE RESEARCH WITHIN SYSTEMATIC REVIEWS

Qualitative research often seeks to interpret, illuminate, illustrate, and explore meaning, context, unanticipated phenomena, processes, opinions,

---

Box 1.1 Ontological and Epistemological Paradigms

Ontologies are theories, assumptions, and beliefs about the nature of social life, of physical entities and realities, and of the self. Questions focus on what can be known about these different forms of existence and what can be assumed about relationships between these "realities."

Post-positivism[1]: Social phenomena are built upon a distinct reality that is independent of the observer.

Interpretivist (or interpretive frameworks)[2]: Social phenomena are intersubjective in their nature and cannot be thought of outside of social or cultural meaning systems. Subjective meanings of reality are constantly changing based on negotiation and revision.

Epistemologies are theories, assumptions, or beliefs about the relationship between the knower or would-be knower, how we can know about the world, and what can be known.

Post-positivism: Supports the application of natural science methods for the search for social reality, which includes deduction, value-controlled methods, hypothesis testing, the use of rigorous statistical and other types of testing, and the search for generalization of knowledge. Knowledge of the external world, although possible, is understood to be incomplete and fallible.

Interpretivist: Supports the interpretive understanding of social actions of individuals and the subjective/intersubjective meanings generated by these social actions, which includes induction, subjective methods, emerging theories, and naturalistic methods for exploring the transferability of knowledge. These frameworks make no distinction between objective and subjective knowledge given that all meaning is understood to be open to reinvestigation or reinterpretation (Pascale, 2011).

[1]Although the term *positivism* is still found in social work textbooks and writings about epistemological approaches in social work, the epistemological paradigm that currently best matches the logical positioning of the natural sciences is *post-positivism*, given its recognition that research cannot be presumed to be value-free, and therefore, the role of the post-positivist researcher is to develop methods to control for these biases.

[2]*Interpretivism* or interpretist frameworks, as philosophical traditions, house a number of different approaches including: *constructionism* (Berger & Luckman, 1966), which proposes that social life, and what can be known about that life, are products of social and symbolic interaction and as such are understood to be only partially known and conditional; and *constructivism*, which proposes that social phenomena are the product of more internally oriented processes. Emphasis here is on understanding how intersubjective experiences are produced and processed cognitively by subjects.

---

attitudes, actions, and to learn about people who are few or hard to reach. Qualitative research "enables researchers to ask new questions, answer different kinds of questions, and readdress old questions" (Fetterman, 1988, p. 17). Such questions are useful when traditional quantitative methods are inadequate for understanding the complexity of a problem, when little

Table 1.1 Comparison of Quantitative and Qualitative Research Approaches

Qualitative Research	Quantitative Research
Assumptions	**Assumptions**
• Reality is socially constructed • Variables are complex, interwoven, and difficult to measure • Emic (insider's point of view) • Ideographic (unique elements of the individual phenomenon)	• Social facts have an objective reality • Variables can be identified and relationships measured • Etic (outsider's point of view) • Nomothetic (search for universal laws)
Epistemological/Ontological	**Epistemological/Ontological**
• Interpretivism	• Post-positivism
Purpose	**Purpose**
• Process-oriented • Contextualization (transferability) • Interpretation • Understanding perspectives	• Outcome-oriented • Generalizability • Prediction • Causal explanation
Process	**Process**
• Ends with hypothesis, theories (inductive) • Emergent design • Researcher as instrument • Naturalistic • Patterns, theories developed for understanding • Few cases, participants • Thematic, discourse analyses • Descriptive write-up	• Begin with hypothesis, theories (deductive) • Manipulation and control • Use formal instruments • Experimentation • Generalization leading to prediction and explanation • Many cases, subjects • Statistical analyses • Abstract language in write-up
Researcher's role	**Researcher's role**
• Personal involvement and partiality • Subjective insider	• Detachment and impartiality • Objective outsider

is known about the research problem, or when researchers do not have adequate information about the context and structures related to a given social phenomenon.

Qualitative methods are also good for pursuing topics that are too sensitive (e.g., emotionally, culturally) for the types of closed-ended questions often asked in quantitative designs (Padgett, 2008). For example, many qualitative data collection methods employed in social work emphasize the interconnectedness between building trust and gathering data over a protracted period of time as a means of bringing a breadth of perspective to the difficult and sensitive experiences being studied. Questions that capture the "lived experience" of those in a particular situation are also better addressed within qualitative inquiry because such inquiries are "*emic*, capturing the respondent's point of view, rather than *etic*, seeking to explain from the perspective of an objective outsider" (Padgett, 1998, p. 8). Evidence derived from qualitative research can not only describe elements of interventions that "work," but can also be helpful in answering questions about why interventions work (or do not work) and the impact that these interventions may have (or do not have) on clients who receive then.

Qualitative research can also be the primary source of data to answer questions that do not focus solely on efficacy or effectiveness (Gough & Elbourne, 2002) but, instead, focus on the experiences and perceptions of clients and the contextual considerations that influence the delivery of services including: the presence of program champions or leaders; the operation and resources for services; the cultural appropriateness, relevance, and sensitivity of services; aspects related to training; and the presence or absence of collaboration among partners in supporting the services. Moreover, qualitative research can address the experiences of nonclient groups, such as social workers (Gearing, Saini, & McNeill, 2007), how systems function socially, such as in the criminal system (Löschper, 2000), and how documentary analysis can provide insight into the creation of socially, legally, and politically dominant discourses (Saini & Birnbaum, 2005).

CONSIDERATIONS FOR INTEGRATING QUALITATIVE RESEARCH WITH EVIDENCE-BASED PRACTICE

Qualitative evidence is important for understanding issues relevant to social workers, yet there remains an on-going debate about the feasibility and merit of integrating qualitative research within the evidence-based practice framework (see Box 1.2).

Moreover, despite the fact that qualitative studies are thriving in social work settings, findings from qualitative methods have remained

---

Box 1.2 Example of the Integration of Qualitative Research within an Effectiveness Study

In 2008, Palinkas et al. published an ethnographic study that explored the implementation of a purportedly effective treatment in a child mental health center. This novel approach of using qualitative research to better understand the process of implementing an effective treatment suggested that trainers, clinical supervisors, and clinicians struggled with the implementation of the treatment as some abandoned the treatment, whereas others considered selective or partial application of the treatment. They also discovered a number of themes that were related to the struggles, including the lag time between initial training in the treatment protocol and treatment use in practice, clinician engagement with the project, clinician–treatment fit, clinicians' first impressions of the treatment after initial use, and competence in treatment use. This qualitative study has important implications for the implementation of effective services within the child mental health context. The findings suggest that simply evaluating the effectiveness of the treatment (whether it works) would not fully capture the context of why it worked or did not work.

---

largely invisible within the evidence-based practice discourse and have had little impact on related clinical practice and policies (Finfgeld-Connett, 2010; Pope & Mays, 2009) (see Box 1.3).

Proponents argue that there is utility for the inclusion of qualitative research findings within evidence-based practice (Jack, 2006) and that qualitative research can contribute to evidence-based practice (Newman, Thompson, & Roberts, 2006) and can also provide yet another important voice in the evidence-based practice debate (Parse, 2007). Sandelowski and Barroso (2002) suggest, however, that there remain a number of barriers to the integration of qualitative research with other forms of evidence. Three of these considerations will be discussed here.

First, there are no steadfast rules or regulations in qualitative analysis. Yet, as Padgett (1998) argues, "such standardization [is not] necessarily desirable" (p. 2). Coffey and Atkinson (1996) further suggest that there is a variety of qualitative research methods "because there are different questions to be addressed and different versions of social reality" (p. 14) and so there is no single methodological framework to guide qualitative research.

A second issue often raised is that there is a lack of consistency with respect to the terminology used to describe qualitative research

Box 1.3 Example of the Integration of Qualitative Research within an RCT

Sibthorpe et al. (2002) describe the challenge of conducting "gold standard" RCTs within marginalized populations. In their study, they attempt to randomly allocate hazardous drinkers in an Indigenous Australian medical health community center to either a brief intervention or usual care. Due to the low participation in the study, the researchers made several revisions to the protocol, including involving Aboriginal people in the screening of potential participants, using non-Aboriginal researchers to screen, and varying the screening tools for eligibility. Although they needed an estimated 400 participants (200 in the intervention, 200 in the control) to conduct the study, only 10 people agreed to participate and none of them indicated that they had a serious drinking problem. Ultimately, the researchers suspended the study, choosing instead to conduct interviews with all relevant staff to identify the barriers of recruitment. The interviews highlighted that patients were embarrassed or resentful about being approached about their drinking, and they did not want to discuss their drinking habits. The interviews with staff also revealed that Aboriginal health workers were too uncomfortable to approach patients about their drinking, many of them felt random allocation was unethical, and they thought the research project was a hassle. Ultimately, the RCT was abandoned, and they wrote to the National Health and Medical Research Council to end their funding.

(e.g., qualitative research, qualitative methods, narrative analysis, narrative inquiry, interpretive research). The word *qualitative* may not even appear in a text, as researchers may use specific qualitative methods to describe their study (e.g., grounded theory, phenomenological approach, discourse analysis, participatory action research). These differences in "naming" the research endeavor make it difficult to locate qualitative studies for inclusion in the synthesis of evidence. Once qualitative studies are located to shed light on a particular question, the inclusion of qualitative research is still a challenge because there are no standardized methods for reporting the design of the study and the pertinent findings are not always clearly stated.

A third objection derives from a misperception about the scientific merit of qualitative findings due to their small sample sizes, irrespective of the value they may bring to understanding the context of the evidence (Finfgeld-Connett, 2010). The aim of qualitative research is not to make generalizations but to develop knowledge from tentative suppositions that describe individual cases (Rodwell, 1987). This is consistent with Sinclair's (2000) notion that qualitative research can provide insight into the complexity of interventions as "qualitative research draws attention to features of a situation that others may have missed but which once seen have major implications for practice" (p. 8). Gaining a rich and complex understanding of contextual factors usually takes precedence over generalizing to other geographical areas or populations. Therefore, many, but not all, qualitative researchers endeavor to employ small samples, principally because they are not concerned with statistical generalizability but rather with conceptual and theoretical development (Pope et al., 2007).

A related concern centers on whether knowledge gained from qualitative studies should remain local or whether the knowledge can be transferred and integrated across studies. In this fourth area of contention, some qualitative researchers argue that the contextual location of knowledge makes transferability undesirable and even inappropriate, whereas others have argued that some shared meanings can emerge from multiple studies even though these meanings can change over time and remain connected to the context of the original studies.

Finally, as we recall, qualitative research is not a single unified tradition but should instead be considered a family of related approaches with different epistemologies and philosophical frameworks (Denzin & Lincoln, 1994; Drisko, 1998; Sherman & Reid, 1994; Tesch, 1990). Epistemology refers to the ways in which we come to "know" something and accept it as "true." Overarching epistemologies relevant to qualitative research include: *post-positive,* which views research as a tool for making conjectures about the general laws of cause and effect operating in social behavior; *interpretive,* which views research as a tool for understanding the myriad of meanings that people ascribe to their lived realities and the different ways these meanings are produced and experienced; and *critical,* which views research as a tool that should be used to improve the conditions of oppressed and marginalized populations (Padgett, 2008). Just like there are many epistemologies relevant to qualitative research, there are as many divergent views about the role and purpose of qualitative research within scientific research. There are some researchers who tend to position themselves in opposition to other worldviews on the paradigm continuum. At the heart of the controversy is a view held by some scholars that the epistemological differences between post-positivistic and interpretive traditions are so great and profound that methods to integrate them are ill-advised and have little scientific merit (Dixon-Woods, Agarwal, Young, Jones & Sutton, 2004). Critics of post-positivism, for example, usually align with Guba and Lincoln's (1989) "fourth generation evaluation" (p. 184) and posit that the world that people create in the process of social exchange is a reality in constant change.

MOVING FORWARD

We respect that there remains little convergence on these matters on either end of the epistemological spectrum, and we acknowledge that some constructivist, interpretivist, phenomenological, and hermeneutic researchers would find even the premise of a synthesis objectionable. Yet, as Dixon-Woods et al. (2004) and others (e.g., see Phillips, 2000) have argued, the perceived irresolvability of the debate between post-positivism and interpretivism can obscure more than it reveals. For these investigators, health inequalities and other disparities, human pain, and the suffering of clients are too great to be ignored on the grounds of philosophical or methodological problems; these debates should not be reason for inaction.

Although we concur with the sentiments behind this plea, we contend that more "pragmatic" approaches to research need not preclude consideration of these research contentions. First, there is a well-established precedent for qualitative researchers to use contradictory evidence within a single study to expand and reformulate theoretical explanations and precepts (Barbour, 1998) and to rely on heterogeneous methods for collecting and analyzing emergent themes and theories (Dixon-Woods et al., 2004). These authors and others (Harden & Thomas, 2005; Padgett, 2008; Pope et al., 2007) suggest that, given current practices within qualitative research, it is acceptable, by extension, to pull disparate sources together to focus on contradictions, exceptions, and similarities across studies while still respecting the diversity of each method. We agree. Put directly, qualitative synthesis, if "presented in an accessible and usable form in the real world of practice and policy making" (Sandelowski, Docherty, & Emden, 1997, p. 365), can enhance our rich conceptual understanding of complex phenomena and, therefore, can influence practice and policy in indirect ways (Denyer & Tranfield, 2007). This linking of scientific knowledge with the experience and judgment of helping professionals is central to an evidence-informed approach.

Second, we contend that where researchers position themselves in relation to these ongoing debates influences their attitudes about the appropriateness of synthesis of qualitative findings and, therefore, we consider it of the utmost importance for researchers to consider their own epistemological and ontological frameworks before embarking on the journey of qualitative synthesis.

Finally, like others in this debate (see Padgett, 2008), we embrace a more pragmatic approach that begins with the research question and explores which method or methods might be best for answering the question. Moreover, as you will read in the following chapters, we stress the importance of understanding the background and rationale for each qualitative research study, as well as the specifics of the method(s) used as a necessary starting point for evaluating qualitative studies. We also argue that careful consideration must be paid to situating the methods in a way that reflects and respects their individual philosophical and epistemological differences.

KEY POINTS TO REMEMBER

- Systematic reviews are the primary vehicle for preparing, maintaining, and disseminating high-quality evidence relevant to social work practice, research, and policy decisions.
- With the large number of completed qualitative studies, the field of social work has a lot to gain by conducting systematic syntheses of qualitative research.
- Qualitative research provides a different type of evidence than quantitative research, exploring individual subjective experiences rather than predetermined categories.
- Qualitative studies can provide in-depth understandings of the experiences and perceptions of people involved in interventions, allow for meaningful explorations of important issues related to implementation and other observable phenomena, and can be used to generate or refute hypotheses.
- Due to differences in philosophical assumptions, strategies for data collection, and methods for analyzing qualitative data,

there are few agreed-on standards within each distinct method for producing high-quality qualitative studies.

- Both qualitative and quantitative approaches to syntheses are considered to be empirical, systematic, and based on scientific inquiry. Qualitative researchers are more likely to follow an inductive approach than the deductive approach prescribed by quantitative designs.
- An understanding of the background and rationale for qualitative research, as well as the method(s) used are necessary to evaluate qualitative studies.
- Careful consideration must be made to capture the various methods of qualitative research and to situate these methods in a way that reflects their individual philosophical differences.
- Some shared meanings can emerge from multiple studies even though these meanings can change over time and remain connected to the context of the original studies.
- There is an urgent need for social work research to find ways to appropriately use knowledge derived from qualitative studies to inform social work policy and practice.

SUGGESTED READING

Systematic Reviews

Dixon-Woods, M., Agarwhal, S., Jones, D., Young, B., & Sutton, A. (2005). Synthesising qualitative and quantitative evidence: A review of possible methods. *Journal of Health Services Research Policy, 10*(1), 45–53.

Mays N., Pope, C., & Popay, J. (2005). Systematically reviewing qualitative and quantitative evidence to inform management and policy-making in the health field. *Journal of Health Services Research Policy, 10*(Suppl 1), 6–20.

Paterson, B. L., Thorne, S. E., Canam, C., & Jillings, C. (2001). *Meta-study of qualitative health research: A practical guide to meta-analysis and meta-synthesis.* Thousand Oaks, CA: Sage.

Pope, C., Mays, N., & Popay, J. (2007). *Synthesizing qualitative and quantitative health research: A guide to methods.* Berkshire, U.K.: Open University Press.

Sandelowski, M., & Barroso, J. (2007). *Handbook for synthesizing qualitative research.* New York: Springer.

Qualitative Research and EBP

Black, N. (1994). Why we need qualitative research. *Journal of Epidemiology and Community Health, 48*, 425–426.

Creswell, J. W. (2006). *Qualitative inquiry and research design: Choosing among five traditions.* Thousand Oaks, CA: Sage.

Maykut, P., & Morehouse, R. (1994). *Beginning qualitative research: A philosophical and practical guide.* London: Falmer Press.

Mays, N., & Pope, C. (1995). Qualitative research: Rigour and qualitative research. *BMJ, 311*, 109–112.

Patton, M. (1990). *Qualitative evaluation and research methods.* Newbury Park, CA: Sage.

Pope, C., & Mays, N. (1995). Qualitative research: Reaching the parts other methods cannot reach: an introduction to qualitative methods in health and health services research. *BMJ, 311*, 42–45.

Wadsworth, M. J. (1998). Designing a qualitative study. In L. Bickman & D. Rog (Eds.), *Handbook of applied social research methods* (pp. 69–100). Thousand Oaks, CA: Sage.

2

Methods for Aggregating, Integrating, and Interpreting Qualitative Research

Several methods for qualitative synthesis have been developed to integrate qualitative studies. The goal of this chapter is to provide an overview of the various methods of synthesis available to the researcher or practitioner based on the perspectives and methodologies of the primary qualitative studies that would comprise a synthesis. These include methods adapted from primary qualitative research methods, (e.g., grounded theory) and others specifically developed for the purpose of qualitative synthesis (e.g., meta-study) (Flemming, 2007). Dixon-Woods, Agarwal, Jones, Young, & Sutton (2005) identified a broad range of methods to synthesize qualitative research including narrative summary, thematic analysis, grounded theory, meta-ethnography, aggregation of findings approach, qualitative meta-analysis, qualitative meta-synthesis, meta-study, Miles and Huberman's (1994) cross-case analysis, content analysis, and case survey. The common link between these different methods is that they all attempt to draw findings across qualitative studies in order to generate new insights and understandings (McDermott, Graham, & Hamilton, 2004).

Before proceeding, however, it is important to note that, despite these attempts to generate different methods for qualitative synthesis, questions remain regarding the ability of any of these methods to adequately capture the contextual nature of qualitative research (McDermott et al., 2004). Abiding tensions within different research communities also exist about the level of analytical attention that should be paid to the epistemological frameworks and the underlying assumptions underpinning both the individual studies being considered for synthesis and methods selected by the researcher (Booth, 2001; Campbell et al., 2003; Murphy, Dingwall, Greenbatch, Parker, & Watson, 1998; Popay, Rogers, & Williams, 1998). Finally, to date, no set guidelines have been developed nor is there even common agreement on the most appropriate method(s) to integrate and synthesize qualitative research findings (Britten et al., 2002).

THE CONTINUUM OF METHODS FOR QUALITATIVE SYNTHESIS

Methods for qualitative synthesis are located along a continuum from aggregative approaches, which involve pooling frequencies of themes across qualitative reports (e.g., meta-summary) to interpretive approaches that construct new interpretations, enhance understanding, and generate new theories about a topic (e.g., meta-ethnography) (Sandelowski & Barroso, 2007). Other more integrative methods lie between these two poles and focus on the propagation of integrated thematic interpretations of an event, phenomenon, or experience (e.g., meta-synthesis). In an attempt to describe this continuum of methods, we provide a decision tree (see Figure 2.1) for choosing a method for qualitative synthesis.

Decisions are based on the following criteria: (a) the epistemological and ontological stance of the researcher; (b) whether the research question is predefined or iterative; and (c) whether the method is aggregative, integrative, or interpretive. If interpretive, then the reviewer needs to make an additional choice of either including comparable studies (e.g., grounded theory, interpretive synthesis) or including different study designs in the interpretation of the findings across qualitative studies (e.g., meta-study, meta-ethnography).

Although we cannot provide an exhaustive explanation of each of these methods and their respective steps within the space available, we have grouped examples of methods according to this continuum to help clarify the relationships between and differences among some of the more common methods for qualitative synthesis. In doing so, we are

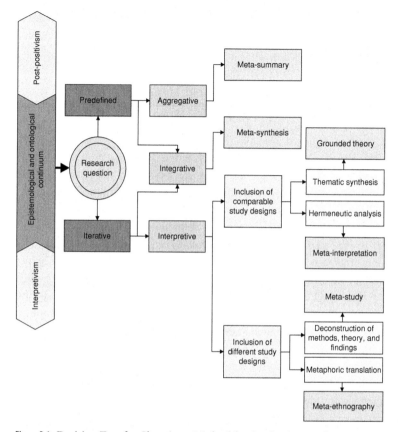

Figure 2.1 Decision Tree for Choosing a Method for Qualitative Synthesis.

cognizant that the boundaries of these methods are permeable and that the typologies are not necessarily mutually exclusive.

Clarifying the differences among qualitative synthesis methods is further compromised because the reporting of qualitative methods has been found to be inconsistent. Bondas and Hall (2007), for example, completed a meta-method study based on a decade of meta-synthesis research in the health sciences and found that it was common for reviewers to make modifications of qualitative synthesis methods without explanation, to provide little information about the procedures used, and to blur the boundaries of the methods by adopting languages across methods to describe concepts and data synthesis strategies. They also found that many studies aggregate findings into meta-summaries instead of interpreting findings across studies, regardless of their chosen method for qualitative synthesis.

PREDEFINED VERSUS ITERATIVE QUESTIONS

Questions explored in qualitative synthesis can be based on either a predetermined understanding of the phenomena or based on an evolving process of discovery. Methods that use predefined questions to guide the review often include well-defined definitions of concepts that can be summarized across studies (Dixon-Woods, Bonas, et al., 2006). Predetermined questions are often defined early in the review process; these are based on prior research, theory, or practice wisdom; and these questions provide the structure for creating themes and categories across studies so that summaries of the findings of each study can be pooled or integrated across studies. For instance, aggregative methods use predefined questions, resulting in descriptive accounts of the findings (e.g., content analysis, meta-summary). By using a set structure of themes and categories based on the predetermined questions, reviewers are able to aggregate the common themes to create an overall description across studies. The reviewer can also use this structure in a more integrative manner to adapt theme and categories across studies as the analysis progresses to provide new interpretations of the data (which may or may not resemble the initial predetermined structure in the analysis). For example, Dixon-Woods, Bonas, et al. (2006) note that within an integrated approach that uses predetermined questions to guide the analysis, the reviewer should not consider these coding structures as fixed, but rather as a starting point for more interpretive ways of considering the findings across studies. Likewise, Sandelowski and Barroso (2007) note that although predefined questions can serve as the focal point of the review, findings can also provide an empirical basis for integrating new interpretations that are located in the analysis and findings, suggesting the emerging process of data analysis and the potential for newly generated interpretations of concepts across studies as the analysis evolves.

Iterative questioning will often avoid specifying concepts or developing fixed meanings about concepts in advance of the synthesis so that the data analysis is grounded in the data and emerges from an iterative process of sifting, sorting, and interpreting the data (Dixon-Woods et al., 2006). In other words, each study within the synthesis is treated as an individual subject, with each generating its own statements in response to questions, and each having its own meanings to be discovered within the synthesis process.

AGGREGATIVE, INTEGRATIVE, AND INTERPRETIVE

As outlined in Figure 2.1, a distinction can be made among the methods according to whether the purpose is to aggregate data, integrate findings, or find new insights and interpretations of the data. Choosing an approach to synthesize qualitative studies will depend on the nature of the research question (predetermined or iterative) and the ontological and epistemological assumptions framing research questions. For example, predetermined questions allow for the creation of common themes across studies, thus facilitating the aggregation of themes. In contrast, iterative questions emerge from the data and are contextually located, thus making the pooling of themes irrelevant.

AGGREGATIVE METHODS

Aggregative methods of qualitative synthesis employ a quantitatively oriented aggregation approach designed to extract, group, and format findings across qualitative studies in a specified research field (Sandelowski & Barroso, 2003b, 2007). Predefined and focused research questions drive the analysis and synthesis (Dixon-Woods et al., 2006; Sandelowski, Docherty, & Emden, 1997). The priority of aggregative methods is often to weight the findings, show the frequency of findings, and provide evidence about the importance of themes across findings. Examples of aggregative methods include meta-summary (Sandelowski & Barroso, 2003, 2007), content analysis (Evans & Fitzgerald, 2002) and case survey (Larsson, 1993). As an example of aggregative methods, we will elaborate on meta-summary developed by Sandelowski and Barroso (2003).

Meta-Summary

Meta-summary reflects a post-positivist approach that views language as neutral, concepts as secure and well-defined, and truth as objective (Dixon-Woods et al., 2006; Sandelowski & Barroso, 2007; Walsh & Downe, 2005). In this sense, all relevant studies are used to maximize the sample size and to provide a more accurate approximation of the frequency counts across the included studies (Finfgeld, 2003) The study designs used within meta-summary include summaries or surveys (topical, thematic) of qualitative research studies and quantitative descriptive findings (Sandelowski & Barroso, 2003, 2007; Sandelowski, Barroso, & Voils, 2007; Thorne, Jensen, Kearney, Noblit, & Sandelowski, 2004). In a meta-summary review, the first step is to read all studies and extract data as part of a meta-level content analysis describing the frequency of themes across studies. Once all data are extracted into codes for descriptive quantitative analysis, results are pooled by calculating the effect sizes and percentages of each theme, and these are then divided by the total number of reports (Sandelowski & Barroso, 2003).

Findings consist of description of the effect sizes and percentage of theme and subthemes reflecting common elements, content, and meaning across studies (Sandelowski & Barroso, 2003). Calculating effect sizes within the meta-summary method involves calculating the frequency of occurrence of an event, and this represents a pattern or theme (Sandelowski & Barroso, 2007). The most frequent findings, based on larger effect sizes or higher percentages, illustrate the most common themes across studies and provide support for each theme across studies. However, less prevalent findings are also assessed for relevance to the overall understanding of the experiences of the participants in the primary studies (Sandelowski et al., 2007). The meta-summary report includes a summary of the data that is then used to highlight connections between studies and serves as an empirical foundation for more interpretive qualitative methods (Sandelowski et al., 2007).

A meta-summary conducted by Martsolf et al. (2010), for example, included 31 qualitative studies to examine aspects of women's and men's responses related to sexual violence survivors' use of professional services. The investigators first coded 271 themes of positive and negative responses then consolidated these into 16 statements. Aggregation of the 16 statements was conducted by calculating a frequency effect size for each of the 16 statements by dividing the number of articles that contained these 16 statements by the total number of articles (n = 31). Martsolf et al. (2010) found that the strongest positive frequency effect sizes related to whether professionals were perceived as competent, providing support, providing acceptance, being nonjudgmental, providing validation of feelings and experience, being present and available, not rushing the client, listening, giving clear information, and providing a safe environment (p. 495). The strongest negative effect sizes related to professionals being perceived as not being present or available, blaming the victim, pushing the client to talk or leave an abuser before being ready, not recognizing client behaviors as being indicative of sexual abuse, giving overwhelming information, having inappropriate sexual boundaries, not allowing the client to direct the therapy including when it ends, being incompetent, and being culturally/racially or gender different from the client (p. 495).

INTEGRATIVE METHODS

Integrative methods for qualitative synthesis, like aggregative methods, are focused on summarizing findings. Similarly, concepts employed to summarize data are assumed to be sufficiently predetermined and well-specified. In contrast to aggregative methods that produce effect sizes or percentages across studies (such as meta-summary), integrative methods create taxonomies of the range of conceptual findings and provide the foundation for the development of conceptual descriptions of phenomena across studies (Sandelowski & Barroso, 2007). For example, Sword et al. (2009) completed an integrated synthesis of women's experiences and perceptions of integrated substance abuse treatment programs. They combined a systematic and iterative process to integrate themes across studies on a number of distinct but interconnected processes that were found to be important to women's addiction recovery, including experiences of individual growth and transformative learning leading to higher quality of life and improved parent–child interactions.

Results such as those reported in Sword et al.'s (2009) study are based on integrative methods considered likely to produce theories of interconnections and causality, and they may also produce claims about generalizability. The objective of integrative methods is to synthesize qualitative findings across studies in order to produce new integrated, descriptive, and explanatory interpretations and perspectives of an event, phenomenon, or experience (Finfgeld, 2003; Sandelowski, 2007; Thorne, 2006; Thorne, Jensen, Kearney, Noblit, & Sandelowski, 2004; Walsh & Downe, 2005). Within this approach, research questions are often guided by previous research and knowledge of topic area (Finfgeld, 2003).

Some have suggested that integrative methods are rooted within post-positive paradigms (Noblit & Hare, 1988); others have argued that meta-synthesis can be situated within a philosophical framework that views knowledge production as meaning-making with an understanding that experiences are both socially and culturally constructed (Sandelowski, 2007; Walsh & Downe, 2005). As a more detailed example of integrative methods, we will elaborate on meta-synthesis as developed by Sandelowski and Barroso (2003).

Meta-Synthesis

Meta-synthesis includes only primary qualitative studies in their sample and extracts concepts, compares and contrasts them, and synthesizes results across studies into taxonomies detailing the range of conceptual findings across studies (Sandelowski, 2007; Walsh & Downe, 2005). Many primary qualitative study designs can be included, such as phenomenology, ethnography, grounded theory, and explanation of phenomena (Sandelowski & Barroso, 2003; Sandelowski, 2007; Thorne, 2006).

Meta-synthesis begins with a predefined research problem and a priori strategies for data collection, inclusion and exclusion criteria, data analysis, dealing with possible sources of bias, and synthesis of findings (Thorne et al., 2004). A set of predetermined questions based on prior knowledge guides the research question for the review. The information retrieval strategy includes all relevant qualitative studies on the topic, regardless of methodological approaches used in the primary studies. The analysis includes reading the findings of the primary studies and extracting metaphors, ideas, concepts, key phrases, and potential relationships of concepts across studies (Sandelowski, 2007; Walsh & Downe, 2005). Meta-synthesis has been described as "the bringing together and breaking down of findings, examining them, discovering the essential features, and, in some way, combining phenomenon into a transformed whole" (Schreiber, Crooks, & Stern, 1997, p. 314, cited in Finfgeld, 2003). When considering the potential relationship of themes across studies, meta-synthesis focuses on findings across studies that are both in conflict and complementary (Walsh & Downe, 2005). The aim of synthesis is to retain the original meaning of each primary study (Thorne, 2006; Walsh & Downe, 2005) while critically analyzing findings between studies for congruencies and similarities, and then reconstructing this amassed data to develop new interpretations that span included studies (Thorne et al., 2004). The meta-synthesis report includes a synthesis of new knowledge through interpreting and refining meanings, concepts, and theories across studies. A recent exemplar of meta-synthesis by Attree (2005) explored the experiences of parents' informal and formal support networks, considering their strengths and weaknesses in the context of poverty and the similarities and differences in parents' accounts of supports across studies. Based on the integration of findings across qualitative studies, Attree (2005) found that although naturally occurring support systems can provide both material and emotional help, these support systems are not universally available for poor parents.

INTERPRETIVE

Interpretive methods involve interpretation of findings across studies to generate new inductive understandings of the phenomena, events, or experiences. Unlike aggregative and integrative methods, which rely on predetermined questions to guide the analysis, interpretive methods use an iterative process to explore what might be involved in similar situations and to understand how things connect and interact (Noblit & Hare, 1988). Clustering toward the interpretive end of the ontological and epistemological spectrum are the methods of meta-interpretation, meta-study, and meta-ethnography (Dixon-Woods et al., 2006). These methods all involve some form of creative process to formulate new constructs by identifying and building on original concepts in the primary studies (Dixon-Woods et al., 2006).

Although there are numerous epistemologies for grounded theory (ranging from traditional questions consistent with post-positivist and novel questions consistent with interpretive or constructivist), we are situating grounded formal theory for data synthesis within the interpretive lens. However, as shown in figure 2.1, we were careful to make links to grounded formal theory via more predetermined questions and approaches in recognition that others may use this approach as an integrative method with an a priori lens rather than the interpretive focus presented in this text.

INCLUSION OF COMPARABLE STUDIES

Reviewers choosing interpretive methods for synthesis will need to make decisions regarding whether to include studies that share similar research approaches or whether to mix different methods. Although there is substantial overlap in interpretive methods, we make a distinction between methods that include comparable studies (e.g., grounded theory, meta-interpretation, interpretive synthesis) and approaches that support different methods within the same synthesis (e.g., meta-study, meta-ethnography). To illustrate an interpretive method of comparable studies, we detail a grounded theory approach to synthesis in the next section, beginning with an explanation of grounded theory as it applies to primary studies and then expanding to synthesis. This method was chosen because grounded theory is one of the most commonly applied methods for primary research, and as such, we presume that more researchers will use this method in their synthesis than other methods.

GROUNDED (FORMAL) THEORY

Grounded theory was first formulated by Glaser and Strauss (1967) and then subsequently expanded upon by Strauss and Corbin (1990, 1998) and Charmaz (1983). *Grounded theory* is a constant comparative method used to generate or discover theory "grounded" in the observed data. Glaser and Strauss (1971) foresaw a time when a substantive body of grounded research would be pushed toward a higher, more abstract level (Flemming, 2007) and thus bring into play the "little islands of knowledge" (Glaser & Strauss, 1971, p. 181) created by each qualitative inquiry. Kearney (1988) introduced the term *grounded formal theory* and suggested that it was best suited to study of phenomena involving processes of contextualized understanding and action (p. 180). Grounded formal theory facilitates the process of synthesis across studies with the lens of producing a broader theory rather than integrating these "little islands of knowledge." Typical research questions relevant to grounded formal theory address common elements across multiple substantive theories that can be synthesized to make a broadly applicable theory regarding observed phenomena. Specific examples include: Eaves's (2001) study on caregiving in rural African American families for elderly stroke survivors; Finfgeld's (1999) study on courage among individuals with long-term health problems; and Kearney's (2001) grounded formal theory of women's experience of domestic violence.

Similar to the original formulation of grounded theory, synthesis includes the process of merging and reducing core categories, core patterns, and themes across studies to facilitate generation of higher level theory and explanations (Finfgeld, 2003; Kearney, 1998; Pope, Mays, & Popay, 2007). Data are systematically extracted (e.g., sample, research question, methods, findings) (Kearney, 1998) and constant comparative methods are used throughout the analysis and interpretation processes to find emerging themes in the data and to consider the interconnections among them. Importantly, given that multiple epistemologies have been linked with grounded theory, including symbolic interactionism, pragmatism, poststructuralism, postcolonial theory, critical reflexivity, feminism, interpretivism, and constructivism (Kearney, 1998; Thorne et al., 2004), Kearney (1998) cautions that depending on the epistemological framework guiding the review, each of these may influence the type and applicability of knowledge derived from the analysis. As such, he suggests that grounded formal theory should be conducted with epistemologically and methodologically consistent research. Moreover, to be included in grounded formal theory, primary studies must be original and use a grounded theory orientation (constant comparative methods, theory development) (Finfgeld, 2003; Kearney, 1998; Pope et al., 2007).

Although including diverse sources that use grounded theory offers more possibilities for theory generation (Bondas & Hall, 2007; Kearney, 1998), such heterogeneity may come with a price. As these investigators note, substantial differences in populations or focus can lead to substantial difficulties when synthesizing across studies.

Syntheses using grounded formal theory often include only grounded theory studies that have explored low level theory with a common sample (e.g., children, parents, or workers) so that rich comparative analyses can be completed to explicate the interconnections between concepts (Kearney, 1998; Thorne et al., 2004). Emerging themes are compared in the primary studies and then compared and contrasted to develop a new theoretical understanding of the data (Kearney, 1998). Data analysis pays particular attention to both the core elements of the participants' responses as well as the contextual factors that may have influenced their responses, such as geographical contexts and temporal framing (Kearney, 1998). These factors, together with theoretical positions found within the primary studies, are harnessed to situate the research across studies (Thorne et al., 2004), resulting in an analysis that is attuned to contextual variations within and between studies. Memoing is often used to record theoretical ideas, assumptions, and analysis decisions as the review progresses (Kearney, 1998). To complete the analysis, categories are explored as they emerge and core patterns and themes are considered across studies to facilitate the generation of midlevel theory (Finfgeld, 2003; Kearney, 1998; Pope et al., 2007). The findings from the analysis are used to develop a central conceptual model mapping the interactions of experiences by explicating the interconnections between concepts and phenomena. Contextual variations within and between studies are accounted for in the final results (Kearney, 1998; Thorne et al., 2004).

As an exemplar of formal grounded theory, Kearney (2001) has synthesized a middle-range theory of women's responses to violent relationships. Descriptive and theoretical analysis included concepts, relationships and stages of women's experiences across a range of personal, sociopolitical, and cultural contexts. Analysis included grounded-theory techniques (Strauss & Corbin, 1998) of substantive coding, which included identifying concepts across studies and clustering them into new categories. Relationships between categories within and across studies were then tested in the data using constant comparative analysis. A theory of normalizing violent relationships emerged in which romance was initially idealized and early violence was discounted for the sake of their romantic commitment. But this pattern shifted toward demoralization with increasingly unpredictable violence and finally, moved toward the creation of a new life.

META-INTERPRETATION

The objective of meta-interpretation is to discover or interpret something new about the human experience instead of verifying what is known or preconceived (Weed, 2005). The first step in meta-interpretation is to identify a research area using an inductive and iterative process, rather than specifying a predetermined question to guide the synthesis. This approach begins with the premise that knowledge is socially constructed and thus varies depending on the different discursive frames orienting that knowledge. Reality is thus understood as being constructed from various vantage points, including the subjective positioning of the reviewer (Weed, 2005). Inherent in this approach is a need for reflexivity and self-awareness of one's epistemology and subjective position in relation to knowledge development. As such, meta-interpretation includes not only the context within the included studies, but also the context in which the research was produced and written (Weed, 2008).

Meta-interpretation does not aim for comprehensive coverage of the literature and, as such, can take a more ideographic approach to the inclusion and exclusion of studies by using theoretical sampling to include studies that are theoretically relevant based on an iterative process of data collection and analysis (Weed, 2008). However, the "aim of theoretical sampling is to refine ideas, not to increase the size of the original sample" (Charmaz, 2000, p. 519). Meta-interpretation is distinguished from formal grounded theory by its emphasis on "meaning in context" and the focus on locating meaning within the context in which they emerge (Weed, 2008). Meta-interpretation draws on Smith, Flowers, and Osborn's (1997) Interpretive Phenomenological Analysis approach that highlights the double hermeneutic process of including the life experiences and views of the world from the interviewees' perspectives and from that of the researcher interpreting these experiences as told to her or him. Weed (2008) suggests that the meta-interpretation approach of synthesis becomes a "triple hermeneutic" when the interpretations of the synthesizer are added to the original research and participant interpretations become the process of "interpretation of interpretations of interpretations" (Weed, 2008, p. 21).

The synthesis of studies begins with a focus on "meaning in context" (Mishler, 1979) involving a holistic and concurrent process of thematic and content analysis of the included studies. During this iterative phase, the synthesizer may exclude studies that are beyond the scope of the synthesis or because the quality of the studies is flawed (Weed, 2008). Following the considerations for inclusions and exclusions into the synthesis, emergent conceptual issues are considered until theoretical saturation has been achieved. Writing the report for the meta-interpretation includes a "statement of applicability" that clearly identifies the boundaries of the applicability of themes that emerge in the synthesis and pays special attention to studies that were included and excluded in the overall synthesis.

Utilizing Weed's (2005, 2008) meta-interpretation approach, Peek Corbin-Staton (2009) explored parental involvement to provide insight into the conceptual and theoretical extensions and differences of parent involvement across qualitative studies. The iterative and transparent methods of data collection and analysis began with a theoretical sensitivity research area of parental involvement and continued until theoretical saturation. Five points of conceptual divergence emerged from the data, namely: protector and nurturer; building positive social relationships; awareness and knowledge; discrete involvement; and parent as learner. The insight gleaned from this meta-interpretation suggest that notions of parental involvement are constructed based on contextual factors of what it means to be a parent and what it means to be involved as a parent.

INCLUSION OF DIFFERENT STUDIES

In the previous section, we focused on interpretive synthesis methods that include comparable studies in their analysis. Other interpretive methods, such as meta-study and meta-ethnography have taken a more pragmatic approach by developing synthesis methods that include different approaches in the inclusion of studies and use this information to assess the potential influence of the various methods and theory on the overall findings. We turn now to a brief explication of meta-study and meta-ethnography to illustrate more encompassing and inclusive approaches to interpretive synthesis.

META-STUDY

Thorne and Paterson (1998), and, later, Paterson, Thorne, Canam, and Jillings (2001) developed the concept of *meta-study* to provide a multifactorial synthesis of primary studies on the basis of theoretical orientation, content, methodology, and contextual notions such as geographical, sociohistorical, and political environments; author discipline; and funding sources (Nicholas, Globerman, Antle, McNeill, & Lach, 2006).

Meta-study can incorporate multiple study designs (Finfgeld, 2003) consistent with interpretive approaches. Meta-study includes a three-step analysis of theory (meta-theory), methods (meta-methods), and findings (meta-data) across studies (Paterson et al., 2001; Thorne, 2006; Thorne et al., 2004). Data, therefore, can include multiple aspects of a report in a specified area of research—study findings, methods, theories, and samples (Thorne, 2006). Meta-theory analysis also involves the scrutiny of the theoretical perspectives of each study, including epistemology, theory, assumptions, and contexts (Finfgeld, 2003; Paterson et al., 2001; Thorne et al., 2004; Thorne, 2006). Paterson and colleagues (2001) asserted that meta-study encompasses not only a systematic review of qualitative research results but also analyzes the inherent sociohistoric, paradigmatic, tangential, and idiosyncratic perspectives imposed on "understandings" of a topic at a given point in time and location (Nicholas et al., 2006).

Within this framework, aligned with a more discursive approach to synthesis (Thorne et al., 2004), the process is reflexive and iterative, and research production is viewed as socially constructed and culturally bound within sociohistorical contexts (Thorne et al., 2004; Thorne, 2006). Meta-study analysis includes all types of primary studies, regardless of their methods, and critically evaluates the rigor and credibility of the particular qualitative methods used to assess the potential influence on the findings. Data analysis includes critically examining the various events, concepts, and phenomena to reveal similarities and discrepancies within and between included studies (Paterson, Thorne, Canam, & Jillings, 2001). The objective of a meta-study is to develop new knowledge, theoretical interpretations, and improved understanding, in part through critically analyzing and synthesizing qualitative studies within the sociohistorical contexts in which they were originally conducted. Integral to meta-study synthesis is an analysis of the synthesis results as also being historically and socially constructed and contingent (Bondas & Hall, 2007; Finfgeld, 2003; Thorne et al., 2004; Thorne, 2006). By considering all included studies, data synthesis is assembled through a type of collage— one that draws attention to the disruptions, fissures, and congruencies— and this disjunctive assemblage provides the terrain from which to create a new, conceptualization reflecting the interpretive tapestry of the three multifactorial synthesis of primary studies (Thorne et al., 2004; Thorne, 2006).

Meta-study was first developed to explore the experiences of adults living with a chronic illness (Paterson, et al., 2001; Thorne et al., 2002). Their findings reveal the complexities inherent not only in any phenomenon of experiences of adults living with a chronic illness but also in the complexities of the accumulated literature over time. Paterson et al. (2001) included a comprehensive information retrieval strategy consisting of qualitative studies published between 1980 and 1996 in any health or social science field that dealt with some aspect of adults' experiences of living with a chronic illness. Data collection strategy capitalized on numerous electronic databases, hand searches of journals, and citation searching. Based on over a thousand research reports, the investigators identified 292 qualitative studies. Meta-theory explored divergent disciplinary and theoretical perspectives that lead researchers to different findings, even if their research questions and sample populations were somewhat similar. For example, Paterson et al. (2001) found that psychologists were primarily focused on psychological implications associated with chronic illness; sociologists focused on the implications of social and cultural structures and expectations associated with illness; and anthropologists tended to focus on patterns of these experiences within larger social and cultural contexts. Meta-method analysis explored divergent findings across different methodological assumptions and structures that shape qualitative findings. For example, psychologists tended to use phenomenology, anthropologists mainly used ethnography, and sociologists focused on grounded theory approaches. Meta-data-analysis was used to explore various conceptualizations, metaphors, and other representations across studies. For example, they found that there were competing metaphors across studies on the nature of the lived experience with chronic illness in terms of the pains and indignities that participants had to endure or the strategies by which they overcame them (Thorne et al., 2002).

META-ETHNOGRAPHY

Noblit and Hare (1988) proposed meta-ethnography as an alternative to meta-analysis in which syntheses of qualitative studies are understood as interpretive rather than integrative or aggregative (Pope et al., 2007). The objective of meta-ethnography is to conceptualize concepts in order to construct new interpretations and enhance understanding (Doyle, 2003; Pope et al., 2007) while acknowledging that alternative understandings and interpretations to the ones generated are possible (Thorne et al., 2004). Sampling of primary studies is purposive as cases are selected for conceptual reasons, not for the generalizability or comprehensiveness of findings (Doyle, 2003; Pope et al., 2007). In other words, learning occurs from a variety of individually selected and unique case studies rather than from an exhaustive list of studies that are systematically appraised and integrated.

Epistemological and ontological assumptions highlight the power dynamics and contextual factors at play within knowledge production across the various approaches to synthesis. Within this approach, meta-ethnography questions claims regarding "truth" (Doyle, 2003; Thorne et al., 2004) and views researcher's perspectives as "always partial and positional" (Thorne et al., 2004, p. 1347). Meta-ethnography reflects Kuhn's position that knowledge production takes place within certain knowledge paradigms, and that argument and counterargument, while contributing to knowledge development, must be understood as amounting to little more than a fine tuning to what is already known (Doyle, 2003; Pope et al., 2007).

Selected studies are based on a selected sample (e.g., only studies involving children are chosen for the synthesis) to better understand a sample's unique experiences. But similar to the meta-study method, studies are not excluded based on the methods used in the primary studies. The review process involves multiple readings of the studies to gain an understanding of concepts and interpretations unique to each selected case study (Doyle, 2003). The synthesis consists of three methods: *reciprocal translation* (translating similar concepts from one study into another); *refutational synthesis* (examining dissimilar components of studies); and *line of argument* (interpreting interpretations to build theory; relating individual study to whole) (Dixon-Woods et al., 2006; Pope et al., 2007; Sandelowski et al., 1997; Thorne et al., 2004). Meta-ethnography follows seven phases that overlap and repeat as the synthesis proceeds: (a) getting started and deciding what the study is going to be about; (b) deciding what is relevant to the initial interest; (c) reading the studies repeatedly, analyzing and noting interpretative metaphors; (d) determining how the studies are related; (e) translating the studies into one another; (f) synthesizing translations to create a new whole of the parts; and (g) expressing the synthesis in written or other form (Noblit & Hare, 1988, pp. 26–29). The meta-ethnographic report includes explanations, new knowledge, and new interpretations generated from the collection of studies. Findings may be different than what emerges from individual studies, and it is this difference that is thought to foster increased critique and dialogue (Thorne et al., 2004).

As an exemplar of meta-ethnography, Wikberg and Bondas (2010) explored intercultural caring of maternity care including prenatal, birth, or postnatal care, or a combination of these. The meta-ethnography method was chosen for its potential "for deriving substantive interpretations about any set of ethnographic and interpretive studies" (p. 9) and the aim of the study was to consider different cultures from an emic view (Wikberg & Bondas, 2010). The sample consisted of 40 articles published between 1988 and 2008 that included more than 1,160 women from more than 50 cultures involved. With few exceptions, the women received care from professionals from another culture. Included studies used a range of techniques for data collection, including observations, field visits, and interviews. The most common methods of data analysis included ethnography, content analysis, and grounded theory. The accounts in the studies were determined to stand in relative opposition to each other and are thus essentially "refutational." Opposite metaphors for maternity care included: caring versus noncaring; communication problems versus choice; preserving one's culture versus adapting to a new culture; and professional caring relationship versus family and community involvement. The overarching metaphor of "Alice in Wonderland" symbolized maternity care in a foreign culture. Intercultural caring was viewed on different dimensions of uniqueness, context, culture, and universality (Wikberg & Bondas, 2010).

SUMMARY

Within the emerging field of qualitative synthesis, there are now a number of methods for answering various questions and handling different types of primary studies. Although the continued growth of qualitative synthesis is expected, so too are the debates about whether qualitative synthesis should be considered a distinct interpretive method or whether progress should be made to find ways to integrate qualitative and quantitative methods within a common set of standards. Weighing in on one side of the debate, Dixon-Wood et al. (2006) argued that incorporating qualitative research into qualitative synthesis remains fraught with challenges. The following may be cited: First, few qualitative synthesis methods have been rigorously evaluated (Dixon-Woods, Agarwal, Jones, Young, & Sutton, 2005), and there remains substantial overlap among them. Moreover, many of the methods highlighted encompass a broad iterative framework, which is often not conducive to providing prescribed methodologies to detail the methods for conducting such reviews. Finally, controversy exists with respect to how to manage, mediate, and address epistemological and ontological positions embraced within individual studies, both across studies and by the individual researcher as she sets out to frame her research questions and the methods that drive them. We cannot hope to resolve these debates here, although we do hold firm in the belief that some questions are better answered using qualitative designs, necessitating a continued expansion in the ways in which we can develop systematic procedures for the inclusion of qualitative research. What we have offered in this chapter, as a means of at least helping to clarify the purpose and objectives of the various qualitative syntheses, is the mapping of these methods within a decision tree. The tree (Figure 2.1), together with Table 2.1, argue for the importance of making central a consideration of questions of ontology and epistemology framing individual studies and driving research synthesis, and the types of research questions that may guide the review process.

Table 2.1 Common Methods for Qualitative Synthesis

Aggregative

Type	Method	Objective	Research Question	Epistemology or Ontology	Data Collection	Study Designs	Review Process/ Analysis	Approach to Synthesis	Output
Meta-summary	To extract, group, abstract, and format findings to determine frequency and effect sizes across qualitative reports. Aggregative.	To produce information; serving as a foundation for qualitative meta-synthesis; informing practice.	Predefined and focused research question(s).	Quantitatively oriented; focused on replication, validity, and uncovering patterns/themes. Reflects a post-positivist approach.	Primary data consists of research findings, typically produced in lists of themes of attitudes and practices. Findings are separated from data. Descriptive findings may be also used from quantitative.	Summaries or surveys of qualitative research studies and quantitative descriptive findings. Report findings by summarizing, rather than synthesizing the data.	The following data is extracted: research purpose, questions, theoretical framework, methods, research design, sampling technique, data collection and analysis strategy, ethics, validity measures, bias measures, and intervention (Sandelowski & Barroso, 2003; Sandelowski et al., 2007)	Empirical findings are abstracted into themes and subthemes reflecting common elements and content. More frequent findings are determined to illustrate evidence of themes and validity; however, less prevalent findings are also assessed for relevance to practice.	To highlight connections between studies and serve as an empirical foundation for a meta-synthesis study.

Integrative

Type	Method	Objective	Research Question	Epistemology or Ontology	Data Collection	Study Designs	Review Process/ Analysis	Approach to Synthesis	Output
Meta-synthesis	Extracting concepts, comparing, contrasting, and reciprocally translating. Interpretive, integrative.	To produce new integrated, descriptive, and explanatory interpretations and perspectives of an event, phenomenon, or experience. To answer questions, develop theory, inform policy, and develop new knowledge.	Iterative Theorizing/ explaining, describing/ characterizing a phenomenon. Research question guided by previous research and knowledge of topic area.	View knowledge production as meaning-making as well as socially and culturally constructed.	Original qualitative data research findings. Include all relevant studies. Transparency in search process.	All qualitative study designs can be included. Studies report findings by interpreting and synthesizing the data.	Meta-syntheses predefine research problem, data collection strategy, inclusion and exclusion criteria, data analysis, possible sources of bias and approach to synthesizing findings. Through reading text and subtext, extract metaphors, ideas, key concepts, key phrases, and relationships in studies. Findings may be conflicting, complementary, or reciprocal.	Empirical, analytical, critical, and/or discursive. To keep the original meaning while deconstructing findings to reconstruct the findings in order to develop new interpretations. Use dialectical and hermeneutic approaches.	Synthesis of evidence. Can be used in cross-disciplinary research teams and designs (Bondas & Hall, 2007). Can develop research hypotheses (Thorne, 2006).

(Continued)

Table 2.1 Common Methods for Qualitative Synthesis (Continued)

Interpretive–Inclusion of Comparable Study Designs

Type	Method	Objective	Research Question	Epistemology or Ontology	Data Collection	Study Designs	Review Process/Analysis	Approach to Synthesis	Output
Grounded formal theory	Reinterpret and integrate data across different qualitative studies examining the same phenomenon. Theory generation and constant comparative methods.	To integrate substantive theory to develop midlevel formal theory to understand and explain phenomenon, processes, and contexts. Understanding grounded in data of meaning, lived experiences, perspectives, and responses.	Iterative. Theorizing/explaining. What is the phenomenon of interest?	Multiple epistemologies linked with grounded theory. Symbolic interactionism. Pragmatic. Poststructuralism. postcolonial theory, critical reflexivity, feminism, interpretivism and constructivism.	Theoretical sampling is used. More studies from diverse sources offer more possibilities for theory-generation. Findings and concepts as well as author's conclusions, interpretation, theory, frame of reference, and discussion may be included as data.	Conducted with epistemologically and methodologically consistent research.	Inductive. Data systematically extracted (i.e., sample, research question, methods, findings). Constant comparative methods include descriptive followed by theoretical coding of data. Memoing may also be used: recording theoretical ideas, assumptions, and analysis decisions.	Core patterns and themes across studies are synthesized. Includes the core element of human responses to a phenomenon and contextual factors that impact this response. A central conceptual model is developed explicating the interconnections between concepts and phenomenon.	New generally applicable formal mid- and high-level theories, explanations, and conceptual models.

Type	Method	Objective	Research Question	Epistemology or Ontology	Data Collection	Study Designs	Review Process/ Analysis	Approach to Synthesis	Output
Meta-interpretation	Involves a triple hermeneutic synthesis. Interpretive.	To generate meaning in context and new understanding and explanations of the essence of a phenomenon. To discover or interpret something new about the human experience instead of verifying what is known or preconceived.	Theorizing/explaining. Iterative and develops with literature analysis.	View multiple socially constructed realities and different kinds of knowledge produced from different methods.	Data retrieval includes finding comparable studies based on theoretical sensitivity and ensuring similar phenomenon in studies.	Can include both published and unpublished original studies.	Data collection forms can be used to extract findings, themes, and categories regarding findings. Hermeneutic analysis, accurately representing findings from individual studies.	Keep unique and holistic nature of each study; compare texts for holistic interpretation. Codes and metaphors are synthesized on a conceptual level to produce a description of the issue.	Applicability statement of relevance and transferability of knowledge to inform practice.

(Continued)

Table 2.1 Common Methods for Qualitative Synthesis (Continued)

Interpretive–Inclusion of Different Study Designs

Type	Method	Objective	Research Question	Epistemology or Ontology	Data Collection	Study Designs	Review Process/ Analysis	Approach to Synthesis	Output
Meta-study	A three-step analysis of theory, methods, and findings across studies is conducted and results synthesized. Interpretive, critical, comparative.	To develop new knowledge, theoretical interpretations, and understanding through critically analyzing and synthesizing qualitative studies within sociohistorical contexts. Goal includes syntheses of social theory.	Theorizing/ explaining/ descriptive. How can we expand knowledge and develop theory within a particular field by conducting a critical sociohistorical analysis?	Developed from sociological theories where data, theory, and methodology are analyzed and synthesized. Critical and discursive approach. View research production and representation as socially constructed and culturally bound within sociohistorical contexts.	Include studies examining research traditions and original studies.	Data can include multiple aspects of a report in a specified area of research: study findings, methods, theories, and samples. Can use multiple study designs.	Inductive. Three-step analysis: (a) meta-data analysis: examining findings across multiple studies; (b) meta-method: examining methodological rigor and epistemology across studies; and (c) meta-theory: examining philosophy, epistemology, theory, cognition, assumptions, contexts. Analysis includes deconstructing research studies using rigorous and systematic methods.	Critical/discursive. Differences, patterns, and methodological inconsistencies are synthesized to create a holistic new conceptualization.	Produce a sociohistorical critique of theories, findings, and methods on a particular topic.

Type	Method	Objective	Research Question	Epistemology or Ontology	Data Collection	Study Designs	Review Process/ Analysis	Approach to Synthesis	Output
Meta-ethnography	Translating concepts from each study into each other through reinterpreting both analytical and theoretical concepts. Interpretive vs. integrative or aggregative. Authors situate themselves in relation to the research.	Reconceptualization and translation of concepts in order to construct new interpretations, enhance understanding, and generate new theory about a topic while acknowledging different understandings and interpretations.	Theorizing/ explaining. Which cases provide "the most opportunity to learn"?	Epistemological underpinnings founded in sociology and critical cultural anthropology. Highlights power dynamics and contextual factors within knowledge production, questions claims regarding "truth."	Purposive sampling; cases selected for conceptual purposes not generalizability or being representative or comprehensive. Can apply boundaries/ inclusion criteria; maximum variation sampling. Data includes original findings, author(s) interpretations, abstract, and title.	Includes different study designs on the same topic, challenging the theoretical approach of meta-analysis or meta-synthesis using similar study designs. Learning from a variety of individually selected and unique case studies.	Inductive approach to analysis. Often iterative and simultaneous translation and synthesis. Multiple readings of the studies to gain an understanding of concepts and interpretations of each selected case study; can use grounded theory to develop metaphors for each study. Stages include: identifying topic, case selection, reading studies, analysis of interrelationships, reciprocal translation, and synthesis.	Empirical, analytic, critical, and/or discursive. Three methods of synthesis: (a) *reciprocal translation* (translating similar concepts from one study into another); (b) *refutational synthesis* (examining dissimilar components of studies); (c) *line of argument* (can be considered: emic, historical, comparative, or holistic.	Novel interpretation developed from findings across individual case studies. May foster increased critique and dialogue.

KEY POINTS TO REMEMBER

- Similar to primary studies, it is often the research question that guides the qualitative synthesis process and frames the chosen method for synthesis.
- The common link between methods for qualitative synthesis is that they all attempt to draw out, integrate, or interpret findings across qualitative studies to generate new insights and understandings.
- A distinction can be made among the methods according to whether the purpose is to aggregate data, integrate findings, or find new insights and interpretations of the data.
- Reviewers conducting interpretive methods of qualitative synthesis should consider whether to include comparable studies or different study designs in the interpretation of the findings across qualitative studies.
- Meta-summary is an aggregative method to extract, group, and format findings to determine frequency and effect sizes across qualitative reports.
- Meta-synthesis is an integrative method for extracting concepts, comparing, contrasting, and reciprocally translating themes across studies.
- Grounded formal theory is an interpretive method that includes a theoretical sensitive sample of studies for reinterpretation and higher order theory generation.
- Meta-interpretation in an interpretive method that explores meaning and involves a triple hermeneutic synthesis.
- Meta-study is an interpretive method consisting of a three -tep process of analysis of theory, methods, and findings across studies.
- Meta-ethnography is an interpretive method for translating concepts from each study into each other through reinterpreting both analytical and theoretical concepts.
- Few methods for qualitative synthesis have been rigorously evaluated and there remains substantial overlap among them.

SUGGESTED READING

Examples of Qualitative Synthesis

Attree, P. (2004). Growing up in disadvantage: A systematic review of the qualitative evidence. *Child: Care, Health and Development, 30*(6), 679–689.

Attree, P. (2005). Parenting support in the context of poverty: A meta-synthesis of the qualitative evidence. *Health & Social Care in the Community*, *13*(4), 330–337.

Barroso, J., & Powell-Cope, G. M. (2000). Metasynthesis of qualitative research on living with HIV infection. *Qualitative Health Research*, *10*(3), 340–353.

Britten, N., Campbell, R., Pope, C., Donovan, J., Morgan, M., & Pill, R. (2002). Using meta ethnography to synthesise qualitative research: A worked example. *Journal of Health Services Research and Policy*, *7*, 209–215.

Greenhalgh, T., Glenn, R., Macfarlane, F., Bate, P., & Kyriakidou, O. (2004). Diffusion of innovations in service organizations: Systematic review and recommendations. *Milbank Quarterly*, *82*(4), 581–629.

Harden, A., Garcia, J., Oliver, S., Rees, R., Shepherd, J., Brunton, G., & Oakley, A. (2004). Applying systematic review methods to studies of people's views: An example from public health research. *Journal of Epidemiology and Community Health*, *58*(9), 794–800.

Jensen, L. A., & Allen, M. N. (1994). A synthesis of qualitative research on wellness-illness. *Qualitative Health Research*, *4*(4), 349–369.

Lemmer, B., Grellier, R., & Stevens, J. (1999). Systematic review of non-random and qualitative research literature: Exploring and uncovering an evidence base for health visiting and decision making. *Qualitative Health Research*, *9*(3), 315–328.

Lloyd, J. M. (2005). Role development and effective practice in specialist and advanced practice roles in acute hospital settings: Systematic review and meta-synthesis. *Journal of Advanced Nursing*, *49*(2), 191–209.

Noyes, J., & Popay, J. (2006). Directly observed therapy and tuberculosis: How can a systematic review of qualitative research contribute to improving services? A qualitative meta-synthesis. *Journal of Advanced Nursing*, *5*(2), 231–249.

Pound, P., Britten, N., Morgan, M., Yardley, L., Pope, C., Daker-White, G., & Campbell, R. (2005). Resisting medicines: A synthesis of qualitative studies of medicine taking. *Social Science and Medicine*, *61*, 133–155.

Saini, M., & Léveillé, S. (2011). Researcher–community partnerships: A systematic synthesis of qualitative research. In S. Léveillé, N. Trocmé, C. Chamberland, & I. Brown (Eds.), *Partnerships in child welfare research* (pp. 1–43). Toronto: Centre of Excellence for Child Welfare.

Sandelowski, M., & Barroso, J. (2003b). Toward a metasynthesis of qualitative findings on motherhood in HIV-positive women. *Research in Nursing and Health*, *26*, 153–170.

Smith, L., Pope, C., & Botha, J. (2005). Patients' help-seeking experiences and delay in cancer presentation: A qualitative synthesis. *Lancet*, *366*, 825–831.

3

Overview of Mixed-Method Systematic Review Designs

In the previous chapters, we focused on the inclusion of qualitative research within qualitative reviews, and we introduced a number of stand-alone methods for integrating or interpreting qualitative studies. We also discussed the inclusion of qualitative research in evidence-based practice as a means to better understand the contextualized experiences, values, and perceptions of clients within an evidence-based practice framework.

In this chapter, we explore some of the steps for conducting multi-method approaches to systematic reviews. Mixed method synthesis designs include both quantitative and qualitative designs. We begin with a brief overview and rationale for conducting mixed-method designs in social work. We then consider the epistemologies and ontologies employed in different research traditions and the possibilities for bridging these differences. The aim is to assess the potential common ground that makes mixed-method designs possible, if not favorable. We then introduce some current attempts to integrate and synthesize qualitative and quantitative research.

Given that systematic reviews have predominantly not only focused on the synthesis of quantitative studies to test the effectiveness of interventions, but have relied on RCTs and quasi-experimental designs, it is not surprising that current literature about mixed methods in systematic reviews remains largely focused on ways to nest qualitative findings within standard quantitative systematic reviews of effectiveness. Moreover, it is important to note that a number of methods for qualitative synthesis presented in chapter 2 have been used in conjunction with quantitative designs, including grounded theory, meta-ethnography, meta-summary, meta-synthesis, and meta-study (Dixon-Woods, Agarwal, Young, Jones, & Sutton, 2004). Although it is beyond the scope of this book to address all methods for mixed-method systematic synthesis of quantitative and qualitative data sources, we will focus on three distinct approaches: (a) Bayesian meta-analysis, (b) realist synthesis, and (c) the Evidence for Policy and Practice Information and Co-ordinating Centre's EPPI approach. Each approach is distinctly grounded in different epistemological frameworks, and each represents a different way of approaching mixed-method synthesis. Bayesian meta-analysis is best situated within a post-positivist framework, as it focuses on the nesting of qualitative studies within quantitative meta-analytic techniques by providing a source of external evidence to inform the choice of variables to be included in the review (Dixon-Woods et al., 2004). Realist synthesis, in contrast, is an interpretive method that includes diverse evidence from both qualitative and quantitative research, as well as materials from newspapers, unpublished reports, statistics, policy papers, and other relevant sources (Pope, Mays, & Popay, 2007). The EPPI approach to synthesis integrates deductive and inductive inquiry by completing parallel quantitative and qualitative analyses to address different but related elements of an overall question.

CONTEXT AND RATIONALE

A substantial literature has been devoted to determining whether mixed methods are possible or whether the ontological and epistemological stances of both traditions are incommensurable (Greene, Caracelli, & Graham, 1989; Greene & Caracelli, 1997; Rossman & Wilson, 1985). Based on a position of incommensurability, purists (both post-positivist and interpretivist) have argued that mixing methods should be avoided due to the differences between objective and subjective realities that cannot converge (Greene, 2008; Howe, 1988). Others have argued that such a position creates an illusion that the two paradigms (objective versus subjective) are mutually exclusive (Sandelowski, 2001).

Mixed-method methodologists have embraced a strand of pragmatism, a philosophical stance that is now (Creswell, 2009) being proposed as the "new orthodoxy" for mixed methods (Quinlan & Quinlan, 2010) and as a "third paradigm" (Johnson & Onwuegbuzie, 2004) to help seal the epistemological cracks created by the perceived philosophical differences of post-positivism and interpretivism (Muncey, 2009). Proponents of this generation of pragmatism argue that social research inescapably requires different perspectives to understand important social questions (Denscombe, 2008; Quinlan & Quinlan, 2010). Although paradigm wars have created a false dichotomy of objective/subjective reality (Muncey, 2009), for these investigators, very few paradigms are pure, single, and distinct. Rather, they are thought to include a mixture of beliefs, perspectives, assumptions, and practices that transform and develop through a continuous emergence of knowledge (Creswell, 2009; Johnson & Christenson, 2008). Although the epistemological differences of post-positivism and interpretivism are recognized, proponents oppose the position that these two orientations are "epistemologically incoherent" (Howe, 1988, p. 10). Within this view, it is difficult, if not impossible, to say where the objective world stops and the subjective world begins (Muncey, 2009).

As mixed-method designs continue to evolve, epistemological and ontological positions will remain an important part of the discourse regarding the benefits and limitations of mixing quantitative and qualitative methods. Tashakkori and Teddlie (2003) concur with this projection, stating that "the field [of mixed methods] is just entering . . . adolescence and [that] there are many unresolved issues to address before a more mature mixed methods research can emerge" (p. 3). Our purpose in highlighting the typologies and paradigms within mixed-method designs is not to resolve the issues, but rather to provide the context needed for social workers considering the potent brew of mixed methods within systematic reviews. We suggest that, given the complexity of phenomena addressed by current social work practice, including more involved client services set within multifaceted policy initiatives, mixed-method designs may very well provide, in certain contexts, an option for "synergy and knowledge growth that mono-method studies cannot match" (Padgett, 2009, p. 104). Yet, given the nascent stage of mixed-methods inquiry and the related controversy of the benefits of such research, we suggest that reviewers would be wise to proceed with caution when considering the possibility of mixing methods within systematic reviews.

BAYESIAN META-ANALYSIS

Bayesian meta-analysis is a quantitative method for data synthesis in which evidence from quantitative and qualitative studies are pooled using meta-analytic statistical techniques (Dixon-Woods et al., 2004). The method begins with a prior estimated size of an effect by describing the plausible potential values for parameter estimates. These parameter estimates are then updated by deriving posterior probability distributions generated through a statistical analysis of the estimates (Egger, Smith, & Phillips, 1997; Voils et al., 2009). In other words, Bayesian analysis begins with a prior belief, based on expert consultation, subjective judgment, and access to external sources of information to assess the prior probability that these beliefs will have an estimated weight or explanatory value with respect to the overall effect when compared with other variables that are included in the analysis. These variables are represented as codes in the analysis. The prior belief about the estimated effect size is then used in conjunction with actual findings to report a final estimate of the weight of the selected codes across the included studies (Dixon-Woods et al., 2004). In Bayesian meta-analysis, confidence intervals will often be wider than those generated by conventional

---

Box 3.1   Exemplar of Bayesian Meta-Analysis

Roberts et al. (2002) conducted Bayesian meta-analysis to identify factors potentially affecting the uptake of childhood immunization in countries of the global north. The final analysis included 32 quantitative and 11 qualitative studies with no exclusion on the grounds of quality. They began by listing, ranking, and weighing factors they believed influenced whether a child received immunizations. Next, they reviewed the qualitative studies, using content analysis, to assess the legitimacy of their initial set of factors. Based on these results, they then updated their beliefs and combined this new evidence to form an estimated prior probability that each factor was associated with immunization uptake. The quantitative evidence was then used to generate the likelihood of immunization uptake, which updated their expert beliefs to create a posterior probability. The results showed common factors in both quantitative and qualitative elements, but also identified two factors in the quantitative results that were not identified in the prior distribution and two factors that had reduced importance but were highlighted as important in the qualitative studies.

meta-analytic techniques because the prior distributions are often based on the subjective opinions of the researcher (Egger et al., 1997).

Bayesian meta-analysis is among the most frequently cited method for synthesizing qualitative and quantitative research findings (Dixon-Woods, Agarwal, Jones, Young, & Sutton, 2005; Voils et al., 2009), but actual examples in the literature are rare (Roberts, Dixon-Woods, Fitzpatrick, Abrams, & Jones, 2002; Voils et al., 2009).

CONSIDERATIONS FOR USING BAYESIAN META-ANALYSIS

Bayesian meta-analysis provides a method for aggregating qualitative with quantitative meta-analysis techniques by helping to identify variables that influence the strength of effect sizes; therefore, it highlights the need to consider qualitative experiences in quantitative methods of inquiry (Dixon-Woods et al., 2004). Several investigators, however, suggest exercising caution in adopting Bayesian meta-analysis. Voils et al. (2009), for example, argue that differences in data collection methods in qualitative and quantitative methods may result in imprecise frequencies associated with each finding. For these researchers, further research is needed to investigate whether findings at the study level, as opposed to an aggregate list of factors at the synthesis level, will prove more fruitful in combining quantitative and qualitative data. Dixon-Woods et al. (2004) suggest that transforming qualitative data into a quantitative form may seem appealing to some segments of the "quantitative community." For others, quantifying the personal experiences of participants will seem problematic and in conflict with the purposes and objectives of gaining in-depth understandings of given phenomena.

REALIST SYNTHESIS

Realist synthesis is a relatively new strategy for synthesizing research. Developed by Pawson and associated colleagues (Pawson, 2006; Pawson and Boaz, 2004; Pawson, Greenhalg, Harvey, & Walshe, 2004), this method of synthesis explores linkages between mechanisms (processes) and outcomes in interventions to better understand "inside workings" of the intervention and its impact on the outcomes (Pawson & Tilley, 1997). In this approach, interventions are understood to consist of a chain of steps (processes) that emerge in a nonlinear fashion. Each stage involves negotiations and feedback, such that the intervention can work as expected, "misfire," or be subjected to modification and change as stakeholders learn and come to understand the intervention and its requisite components. Realist synthesis can help to better understand the plurality of evidence by supporting each of the linkages that connect interventions.

Realist synthesis follows a heterogeneous and iterative process, which is less prescriptive than a traditional systematic review. For Pawson (2006), a realist synthesis consists of a six-step process (see box 3.2).

Box 3.2   Steps in Realist Review (Adapted from Pawson & Boaz, 2004)

Step 1: Clarify scope
- Identify the review question including the nature and content of the intervention and its use.
- Refine the purpose of the review by mapping the territory.
- Articulate key theories to be explored and formalize the model.

Step 2: Search for evidence
- Exploratory search of the literature.
- Progressive focusing to identify key program theories; refining inclusion criteria in light of emerging data.
- Purposive sampling to test a defined subset of these theories with additional "snowball" sampling to explore new hypotheses as they emerge.
- Final search for additional studies when the review is near completion.

Step 3: Appraise primary studies
- Use judgment to supplement formal critical appraisal checklists and consider relevance and rigor.

Step 4: Data extraction
- Develop data extraction forms and notation devices.
- Extract different data from different studies to populate evaluative framework with evidence.

Step 5: Synthesize evidence and draw conclusions
• Synthesize data to achieve refinement of program theory.
• Allow purpose of review to drive the synthesis process.
• Use "contradictory" evidence to generate insights about the influence of context.
• Present conclu.sions as a series of contextualized decision points of the general format "If A, then B" or "In the case of C, D is unlikely to work."

Step 6: Disseminate, implement, and evaluate
• Draft and test out recommendations and conclusions with key stakeholders.
• Work with practitioners and policymakers to apply recommendations in particular contexts.
• Evaluate in terms of the extent to which programs are adjusted to take account of contextual influences revealed by the review. The same program might be expanded on in one setting, modified in another, and abandoned in yet another.

Stage 1 involves identifying the review questions, mapping the territory (concept mining), prioritizing the review questions, and formalizing theory for the review. Stage 2 includes a background search of the literature (e.g., gray literature search, interviews with "experts") to help map the territory, a search for literature that describes program theories, a search to locate empirical evidence that tests these theories, and a final search to fine-tune the synthesis. Developing the focus of the study and the theories to be examined are important aspects of a realist synthesis (Pawson et al., 2004), as they provide the structure for examining a diverse body of information. Stage 3 consists of quality assessment of the literature for both relevance and rigor. Stage 4 involves extracting the data by using techniques such as annotation and collation of included documents. Synthesizing the data occurs at stage 5 and focuses on the program integrity, comparative analysis of theory among interventions, and comparing official expectations with actual practice. The last stage (stage 6) involves dissemination of results by using knowledge translation methods for the coconstruction of knowledge use and application.

CONSIDERATIONS FOR USING REALIST SYNTHESIS

Realist synthesis can accommodate multiple types of evidence, including both qualitative and quantitative research (Pope et al., 2007) (see box 3.3). How this information is integrated is less clear and further development is needed. There is also a tendency to treat all forms of evidence collected as equally authoritative (Dixon-Woods et al., 2005). Moreover, there is, as yet, no single approach for assessing rigor across these various sources nor is there agreement on how to treat variation of rigor in the analysis

---

Box 3.3 Exemplar of Realist Synthesis

O'Campo et al. (2009) undertook a realist synthesis in collaboration between academic and community-based partners to explore program approaches and program elements that lead to improvements in mental health and substance-use disorders among homeless individuals with concurrent disorders. The investigators note that the literature in this area was characterized by poor evaluation designs with a focus on short-term follow-up and a wide range of interventions employed with heterogeneous populations.

Using an iterative approach, the investigators first identified the topic and scope of the review by narrowing the population to people who are homeless. This decision was heavily influenced by the evidence needs of the community partners who sought to improve their services.

Step 2 consisted of a search of scholarly, peer-reviewed literature on concurrent disorders using relevant medical and social science databases. The 17 peer-reviewed articles (both quantitative and qualitative) that were ultimately included in the review discussed 10 community-based interventions geared specifically to clients with concurrent disorders who were experiencing homelessness, with evaluations assessing outcomes related to mental health or substance-use disorders. In addition, literature describing programs located in the community were included and incorporated. Other sources included gray literature, e-mailed correspondence and interviews with authors of included studies, and qualitative program description information gleaned from supplementary literature or through communications with the corresponding authors.

Step 3 involved quality appraisal by examining methodological rigor (e.g., sample size and statistical power, presence and strength of the comparison group, use of sound outcome measures, recruitment of the sample of homeless persons). The investigators do note, however, that quality appraisal was conducted on a case-by-case basis during the literature search, extraction, and synthesis process.

Step 4 included data extraction of the available data (e.g., statistical power, sampling strategies, strength of the comparison groups and methods of evaluation, internal and external validity). The team assessed the level of statistical power available in the study and employed power calculations using information on reported differences between treatment and comparison groups and the sample size available for the analyses. To assess the rigor of the evaluation design, the team assessed the presence of, or appropriateness and comparability of, the comparison groups as well as the recruitment strategies to determine whether relevant sources of bias could have been introduced. To address the quality of evidence available to determine what works and why, the team considered whether the studies presented sufficient descriptions of the program components and their mechanisms according to quality appraisal techniques.

Step 5 involved data synthesis.

Step 6 involved dissemination strategies including the continuous involvement of community-based agencies in various stages of the research processes. The team was particularly motivated to retain involvement of these key stakeholders to maximize the chance that the evidence would be used to change or inform current practice or policy.

Through a review of the available evaluative and qualitative descriptive evidence, the team identified six promising program strategies for the improvement of concurrent disorders, including: an emphasis on client choice in treatment and decision making, positive interpersonal relationships between the client and provider, assertive community treatment approaches, providing independent housing along with other services, providing services beyond mental health and substance-use treatment, and nonrestrictive program approaches.

(Pope et al., 2007). Although the method provides robust information about the theory being evaluated, Dixon-Woods et al. (2005) note that there is a lack of explicit guidance on how to deal with contradictory evidence, as all evidence is considered equal.

THE EPPI APPROACH FOR COMBINING SEPARATE SYNTHESES

The Evidence for Policy and Practice Information and Co-ordinating Centre (EPPI-Centre) is part of the Social Science Research Unit at the Institute of Education, University of London. The EPPI-Centre conducts systematic reviews across a range of topics and works with a large number of funders in the areas of education, health promotion, employment, social care, and crime and justice. In addition, the EPPI-Centre develops methods in social science and public policy for systematic reviews. One major area of work has been the development of methods for combining different types of evidence and reviews that contain more than one synthesis to explore different types of questions (Harden & Thomas, 2005). The method of combining separate synthesis to answer both broad questions and subquestions is a departure from traditional systematic reviews that use a single method (e.g., meta-analysis) to answer a single question (e.g., does the intervention "work"?). The EPPI-Centre's method includes two or more parallel systematic syntheses that focus on effectiveness, appropriateness, barriers, and enablers to the implementation of an intervention and the views of potential, current, and/or past users targeted by the intervention (Pope et al., 2007). The main steps of the EPPI-Centre method are shown in Figure 3.1. The EPPI method

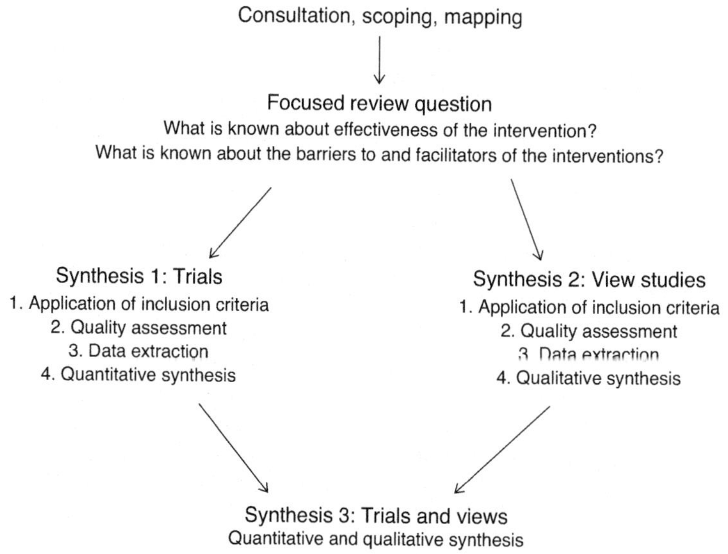

Consultation, scoping, mapping

Focused review question
What is known about effectiveness of the intervention?
What is known about the barriers to and facilitators of the interventions?

Synthesis 1: Trials
1. Application of inclusion criteria
2. Quality assessment
3. Data extraction
4. Quantitative synthesis

Synthesis 2: View studies
1. Application of inclusion criteria
2. Quality assessment
3. Data extraction
4. Qualitative synthesis

Synthesis 3: Trials and views
Quantitative and qualitative synthesis

Figure 3.1 Main steps in EPPI Centre review of mixed-method evidence. Reprinted from Methodological issues in combining diverse study types in systematic reviews by A. Harden and J. Thomas, 2005, *International Journal of Social Research Methodology*, 8(3), 257–271. Copyright 2005 by Taylor and Francis.

includes all of the traditional steps of a systematic review, but intervention studies (e.g., RCTs) and nonintervention studies (e.g., qualitative interviews) are first synthesized separately before integrating the two approaches into a mixed-method synthesis (Harden & Thomas, 2005) (see box 3.4).

Box 3.4   Exemplar of the EPPI Approach

The broad question and subquestions for this review conducted by Harden and Thomas (2005) included: "What is known about the barriers to, and facilitators of, healthy eating among children aged 4–10 years?" (p. 1010) and the specific questions focused on the intake of fruits and vegetables. The mixed-method synthesis included two parallel sets of stages in the review process: controlled trials (randomized or nonrandomised) that examined interventions to promote healthy eating and qualitative studies to explore children's perspectives and understandings of fruit and vegetable intake. Both arms of the synthesis used traditional systematic review methods for information retrieval, screening and classifying studies, and both were assessed for quality according to the relevant standards for each study type (Harden & Thomas, 2005).

For the intervention studies, meta-analysis was conducted to assess effect sizes for the effectiveness of interventions to promote children's increased intake of fruits and vegetables. For the qualitative studies, textual data were entered into QSR International's NVivo (Melbourne, Australia), a software package to aid qualitative analysis.

Qualitative synthesis was conducted by aggregating findings across studies to explore common themes obtained from the children's experiences.

The synthesis then integrated both qualitative analysis and statistical analysis by developing a matrix. As stated in Thomas, Harden, et al., (2004, p. 1011), three questions guided this analysis: "Which interventions match recommendations derived from children's views and experiences?"; "Which recommendations have yet to be addressed by soundly evaluated interventions?"; and "Do those interventions that match recommendations show bigger effect sizes and/or explain heterogeneity?" Thus, the product of the "views" synthesis was the mechanism for combining the findings of the trials studies. Matches, mismatches, and gaps were identified.

The statistical analysis involved comparing the effect sizes from interventions that matched children's views to those that did not using subgroup analysis (e.g., comparing interventions emphasizing health messages to those that had little or no emphasis on health messages).

By completing this subanalysis, they found that the only studies to increase children's vegetable consumption had little or no emphasis on health messages. In other words, in order to increase children's vegetable consumption, do not target health messages at children. Try something a bit more engaging! Although this conclusion may seem obvious to anybody with children, a simple reliance on RCTs would not have uncovered this finding and the opportunity for developing more effective interventions might have been lost.

CONSIDERATIONS FOR THE EPPI APPROACH

The EPPI approach has a number of advantages compared with other methods for integrating quantitative and qualitative methods, and it is the method most congruent with our vision of integrating qualitative methods within systematic reviews. First, the parallel synthesis of quantitative and qualitative studies fits best with conventional methods for conducting comprehensive and transparent systematic reviews. Like traditional systematic reviews, it focuses on exhaustive information retrieval strategies for searching and screening potentially relevant studies, and it follows conventional methods for conducting meta-analysis of quantitative data. The EPPI approach further advances the relevance of systematic reviews with the additional emphasis on including other types of studies to answer questions not amenable for quantitative analysis strategies. This approach can involve any number of parallel forms of evidence that might influence the robustness of the effects of the intervention, including perceptions of participants, processes and mechanics of interventions, accessibility issues, potential barriers for implementation, recruitment difficulties, and the feasibility of the interventions (Pope et al., 2007). The parallel approach to synthesis facilitates the contribution of both quantitative and qualitative evidence within a systematic review by focusing on different but related questions within a review and focusing on the method that can best answer a particular question or subquestion. The parallel method also provides an approach where quantitative and qualitative methods can each be assessed based on quality appraisals that are relevant to each approach. The integration of synthesis then allows new knowledge to be derived based on a consideration of both quantitative and qualitative studies, so neither needs to be nested within the other and both can be fully utilized in the creation of knowledge.

SUMMARY

Similar to mixed-method designs of primary studies, there is a growing interest in conducting mixed-method synthesis using both quantitative and qualitative procedures to synthesize empirical research (Harden & Thomas, 2005; Sandelowski, Voils & Barroso, 2006). Yet, as we have discussed, many unanswered questions as to how to integrate qualitative and quantitative evidence remain (Dixon-Woods et al., 2005) thus making it difficult to explicitly guide researchers attempting to employ mixed-method designs for systematic synthesis. In considering a way forward, we conclude this chapter by referencing three specific dimensions identified by Leech and Onwuegbuzie (2009) for conducting mixed-method primary studies that we believe can be fruitfully adapted for mixed-method syntheses. These targeted challenges include: (a) the level of mixing (separate synthesis, partial mixing, or full integration); (b) time orientation (sequential or concurrent); and (c) the status given to each method (equal status or dominant status). As new methods emerge for mixed-method synthesis in systematic reviews, each of these three dimensions will need to be explored and a clear rationale made for each.

KEY POINTS TO REMEMBER

- Researchers are increasingly turning to mixed-method approaches to address the practical challenges and uncertainty arising from the limitations of using single methods to understand complex phenomena.
- As mixed-method designs continue to evolve, epistemological and ontological positions will remain an important part of the discourse regarding the benefits and limitations of their use.
- Mixed-method strategies will continue to evolve and new developments will be made that respect the strengths of both quantitative and qualitative designs while embracing their complementary differences.
- There is a growing interest in conducting mixed-method systematic synthesis, and this parallels the growing interest in the field for conducting mixed-method primary studies.

- Bayesian meta-analysis is a quantitative method for data synthesis in which evidence from quantitative and qualitative studies are pooled using meta-analytic statistical techniques.
- Realist synthesis explore linkages between mechanisms (processes) and outcomes in interventions to better understand the "inside workings" of the intervention and its impact on the outcomes.
- The EPPI-Centre's method includes two or more parallel systematic syntheses that focus on effectiveness, appropriateness, barriers, and enablers to the implementation of an intervention and the views of potential, current, and/or past users targeted by the intervention.
- Researchers have largely focused their efforts on the synthesis of quantitative studies used to test the effectiveness of interventions. However, mixed syntheses have been conducted and some (notably Harden and Thomas'[2005] EPPI study) have successfully added to the knowledge base in given areas in ways that would not otherwise have occurred.
- At this point, the EPPI approach appears to be the most rigorous and well-developed of the three mixed-method designs focussed on in this chapter.

SUGGESTED READING

Evans, D., & FitzGerald, M. (2002). Reasons for physically restraining patients and residents: A systematic review and content analysis. *International Journal of Nursing Studies, 39,* 735–743.

Harden, A., Oakley, A., & Oliver, S. (2001). Peer-delivered health promotion for young people: A systematic review of different study designs. *Health Education Journal, 60,* 339–353.

Roberts, K., Dixon-Woods, M., Fitzpatrick, R., Abrams, K., & Jones, D. R. (2002). Factors affecting uptake of childhood immunisation: A Bayesian synthesis of qualitative and quantitative evidence. *Lancet, 360,* 1596–1599.

Stephenson, J. M., Imrie, J., & Sutton, S. R. (2000). Rigorous trials of sexual behaviour intervention in STD/HIV prevention: What can we learn from them? *AIDS, 14*(Suppl 3), S115–S124.

Thomas, J., Harden, A., Oakley, A., Oliver, S., Sutcliffe, K., Rees, R., . . . Kavanagh, J. (2004). Integrating qualitative research with trials in systematic reviews. *BMJ, 328*(7446), 1010–1012.

4

Clarifying Methodological Issues: A Way Forward

Although there are a number of qualitative researchers who support the development of methods that integrate knowledge across studies, these same investigators also acknowledge that the broad term *qualitative research* includes diverse commitments to various disciplines, philosophical assumptions, theoretical frameworks, political ideologies (Sandelowski & Barroso, 2007), and that these differences can create epistemological and ontological tensions when attempts are made to build common frameworks for the purpose of integration. Paying heed to these debates, our overall contention is that care must be taken not only when considering the different types of methods used in the studies that are synthesized, but also when considering the various controversies framing questions of assessing the quality of studies to be included. In this chapter, we briefly highlight key methodological challenges that are worthy of consideration for any researcher, policymaker, and practitioner interested in engaging in this type of research. Emerging out of this discussion is a presentation of a series of methodological propositions that will be considered foundational to the model that we propose in chapter 5.

KEY CHALLENGES

Generalizability of Qualitative Synthesis

With the development of both stand-alone and mixed-method designs for qualitative synthesis, a new era in generalizable qualitative theory has begun (Bondas & Hall, 2007; Finfgeld-Connett, 2009). Given the strong philosophical positions about the nature and use of knowledge, readers may question our proposed use of the term *generalizability* to describe findings gleaned from qualitative reviews because it is a term most associated with statistical generalizability within quantitative designs. Generalizability is often linked with *nomothetic science* (the search for universal laws), whereas qualitative research has been viewed as *idiographic* (a perspective that considers knowledge as contextual and situational) (Baskerville & Wood-Harper, 1996). Although nomothetic and idiographic sciences have been viewed as dichotomously opposed, Finfgeld-Connett (2009) suggests these sciences lie on a continuum. That is, one should not think of generalization as an either/or proposition. Studies are never perfectly generalizable to a population if they employ any kind of sampling method. Even the most rigorous quantitative studies provide only estimates. Qualitative research, due to the sampling methods employed (e.g., generally nonrandom sample selection, small samples) tend to fall on the less generalizable end of the continuum. Such a view is held by a great number of qualitative researchers, even if it is not acknowledged. For example, although qualitative researchers frequently reject generalizations, it is not uncommon for qualitative studies to include clinical implications suggesting how their findings might be used outside of the settings in which they originally emerged, nor is it uncommon for qualitative researchers to use quantitative studies as "evidence" of a problem in their literature reviews and discussions! Qualitative synthesis, which includes a collection of these types of "moderate generalizations" (Finfgeld-Connett, 2010, p. 248), moves qualitative findings along the continuum of generalization.

Transparency

Qualitative synthesis methods have been distinguished by their flexible methods and iterative processes for collecting, extracting, appraising, and synthesizing qualitative studies (Pope, Mays, & Popay, 2007).

Although flexibility seems to be a common theme across most qualitative synthesis methods, it is more pronounced in some methods (e.g., realist synthesis) than others (e.g., Bayesian meta-analysis). However, issues of flexibility should not detract from, nor be viewed as, a suitable substitute for the need to address transparency. Transparency of methods and the decisions made by the research team can increase the quality of syntheses and assist in the transferability of findings (Denyer & Tranfield, 2006).

Transferability of Qualitative Synthesis

As the field grapples with the potential generalizability of knowledge gained from qualitative synthesis, it is equally important to consider transferability from one context to another. Complementing the propositions for transferability set forth by Lincoln and Guba (1985), Finfgeld-Connett (2009) propose a framework in which it is the consumer (researcher, clinician, client) who takes primary responsibility for deciding on transferability, because the reviewer cannot be familiar with all potential implementation scenarios. Essential to this formulation, is the transparency of qualitative methods so that consumers of this "new knowledge" are fully informed about the process, context, and situations of the qualitative synthesis in order to make judicious decisions about the transferability of findings (Lincoln & Guba, 1985). With an emphasis on transparency, it is likely that new methods will begin to emerge that assess the rigor and quality of systematic reviews using qualitative research to enhance the transferability of findings from qualitative synthesis.

Posing Research Questions

There are divergent views on how precise the questions should be when developing methods for qualitative synthesis and whether a review should start with an a priori question to guide the analysis (Dixon-Woods, Agarwal, Young, Jones, & Sutton, 2004). Harden and Thomas (2005) suggest that reviewers should first consider the types of questions that the review will address and then plan the review accordingly. Others argue that phenomena should naturally emerge throughout the process of searching, collecting, and synthesizing the data (Jensen & Allen, 1996). We have taken the position that different methods are best used for different types of questions. In this way, a clear and well-defined question helps to determine which method might best address a particular problem, issue, or area of interest. Further, given that posing a well-built question of relevance to clients is one of the hallmarks of evidence-based practice (Sackett, Rosenberg, & Gray, 1996; Gibbs, 2003), questions of precision and sequencing are always in the mix.

Information Retrieval/Sampling of Studies

As methods for qualitative synthesis develop, researchers are continuing to advance techniques for searching for qualitative studies (Flemming, 2007). At issue remains whether to use a comprehensive search strategy to locate all relevant studies, which are consistent with conventional systematic reviews, or to sample selected studies guided by theory. As noted by Schreiber, Crooks and Stern (1997) and Dixon-Woods et al. (2004), deciding on a method of searching will depend on the question(s), the desired product, and the ontological and epistemological framework for the analysis. Within an approach that treats synthesis of qualitative research as part of the overall family of systematic reviews (such as the one proposed in this book), comprehensive, exhaustive, and systematic methods for information retrieval are used to produce the most transparent and credible sources of information for a particular question. Once all sources have been identified, then the reviewer is faced with the difficult challenge of screening, appraising, and classifying. From this list of relevant sources, sampling of particular qualitative studies can occur while still remaining consistent with notions of theoretical sampling. We share similar concerns as Jensen and Allen (1996) and Sherwood (1999) that selective sampling too soon in the information retrieval process may result in the omission of relevant data, thereby limiting the exploration of relevant phenomena and the context in which they occur (Dixon-Woods et al., 2004).

Critical Appraisal

Given the divergent methods in qualitative research, our broad-based appraisal form that we have developed (see chapter 6) assesses the overall congruency of selected methods. In this view, not only is there no previously established hierarchy of qualitative methods (grounded theory is no better or worse than ethnography, for example), but the "best" method is determined by a number of factors including the question being asked, the context of the study, resources, and the philosophical paradigm guiding the approach. Moreover, rather than focus on each method individually, we suggest that an appraisal form can assess quality across methods when quality is assessed by the congruency and consistency of the basic elements of each respective method, as well as a level of transparency that makes an assessment of transferability of experiences possible.

MOVING FORWARD

For qualitative synthesis to provide interpretation and guidance for understanding contextual factors germane to qualitative research, more attention is needed to ensure that the information retrieval strategies are comprehensive, sampling strategies of included qualitative studies are transparent, heterogeneity of quality is addressed, and exaggerated contextual interpretations are avoided within the systematic review process (Jensen & Allen, 1996).

Based on our experiences of using the best available evidence to answer different research questions, we propose a systematic synthesis approach in chapter 5 that enhances transparency, consistency, and rigor while still responding to the central philosophical challenges of including qualitative studies. Careful attention is made to present an approach whereby studies are grouped with similar epistemological and ontological frameworks to promote philosophical consistency throughout the synthesis process. The approach is presented with enough information about the controversies to allow readers an opportunity to form their own opinion and to provide the information they need to avoid some of the major philosophical and methodological pitfalls they will surely encounter.

KEY POINTS TO REMEMBER

- The transparency of qualitative methods ensures that consumers of this "new knowledge" are fully informed about the process, context, and situations of the qualitative synthesis in order to make judicious decisions about the transferability of findings
- Different methods are best used for different types of questions.

- Deciding on a method of searching will depend on the question, the desired product and the ontological and epistemological framework for the analysis.
- Our broad-based appraisal form assesses the overall congruency of selected methods.
- We propose a systematic synthesis that enhances transparency, consistency, and rigor while still responding to the central philosophical challenges of including qualitative studies.

SUGGESTED READING

Dixon-Woods, M., Agarwal, S., Jones, D., Young, B., & Sutton, A. (2005). Synthesising qualitative and quantitative evidence: A review of possible methods. *Journal of Health Services & Research Policy, 10*(1), 45–53b.

Mays, N., Pope, C., & Popay, J. (2005). Systematically reviewing qualitative and quantitative evidence to inform management and policy-making in the health field. *Journal of Health Services & Research Policy, 10*(Suppl 1), 6–20.

Paterson, B. L., Thorne, S. E., Canam, C., & Jillings, C. (2001). *Meta-study of qualitative health research: A practical guide to meta-analysis and meta-synthesis.* Thousand Oaks, CA: Sage.

Pope, C., Mays, N., & Popay, J. (2007). *Synthesizing qualitative and quantitative health research: A guide to methods.* Berkshire, U.K.: Open University Press.

Part II

A Systematic Approach to
Qualitative Synthesis

5

Systematic Synthesis of Qualitative Research

SYSTEMATIC ANALYSIS OF QUALITATIVE STUDIES WITHIN SYSTEMATIC REVIEWS

In previous chapters, we have presented arguments for the inclusion of qualitative synthesis within the "family of systematic reviews" (see Figure 5.1), given that it is both a unique method for answering research questions, as well a method that compliments and enhances other methods. Moreover, as we recall from these chapters, systematic reviews are described as an overarching approach that includes reviews of evidence on a clearly formulated question using explicit methods to identify, select, and critically appraise relevant primary research that includes a transparent and systematic process of extracting and analyzing data from studies. Finally, we have argued that reviewers need to be cognizant of the specific ontological and epistemological frameworks, as well as the objectives, purposes, data collection techniques, and analytic approaches of their chosen method in order to remain consistent with their chosen method of synthesis.

In this chapter, we present an outline of a working approach for conducting a systematic process for collecting, screening, and classifying sources based on whether studies are considered quantitative or qualitative by design. To illustrate the applicability of our approach, we first introduce a systematic review on family group decision making (FGDM)

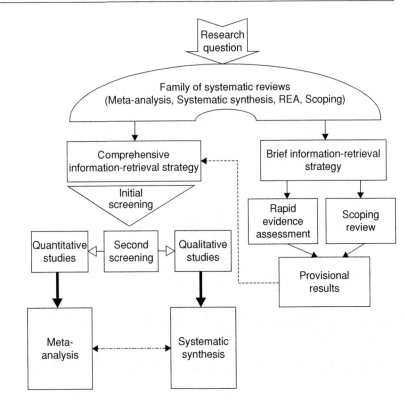

Figure 5.1 The Systematic Review Family.

within a child-protection context (see box 5.1). The 11-step approach for conducting systematic synthesis of qualitative research (Figure 5.2) is then highlighted in the remainder of this chapter and explored more fully in subsequent chapters. Lessons gleaned from the case study will be referred throughout to illuminate various steps.

STEPS FOR CONDUCTING A REVIEW WITHIN THE FAMILY OF SYSTEMATIC REVIEWS

Step 1: Determine the Research Question

The first step in planning for a systematic review involves selecting a topic to be reviewed. In our view, systematic reviews should clearly

---

Box 5.1   Family Group Decision Making

Family group decision making for children at risk of abuse and neglect. Protocol Co-registered with Campbell and Cochrane Collaborations. Review forthcoming.

The Intervention

Family group decision making (FGDM) is a "family-centered" approach. Families are considered "experts" and contribute to plans designed to promote the safety and well-being of their children (Cunning & Bartlett, 2006). A central objective is to provide the family with a stronger voice in decision making than has typically been the case in traditional (often adversarial) child-protection services. FGDM models have been widely implemented in several countries, including: New Zealand, United Kingdom, Canada, United States, Australia, France, South Africa, Sweden, Norway, Denmark, Israel, and the Netherlands (Cashmore, 2000; Goldstein, 2006). There is widespread support and investment in FGDM interventions. However, key outcomes for children (safety, permanence, and well-being) and families who receive FGDM interventions are not well known (Connolly, 1994, 2004; Maluccio & Daly, 2000; Sundell & Vinnerljung, 2004). Little is also known regarding the experiences of children and families who receive FGDM interventions. No quantitative or qualitative review has systematically synthesized existing research.

Objectives of the quantitative meta-analytic analysis

To assess the effectiveness of the formal use of FGDM in terms of child safety, permanence (of child's living situation), child and family well-being, and client satisfaction with the decision-making process.

Objectives of the qualitative meta-synthesis

To explore and to synthesize knowledge from qualitative investigations of family decision making within the context of child protection.

Adapted from Shlonsky, A., Schumaker, K., Cook, C., Crampton, D., Saini, M., Backe-Hansen, E., & Kowalski, K. (2008). Family group decision making for children at risk of abuse and neglect. Co-registered with Campbell Collaboration and Cochrane Collaboration Systematic Review Protocols. (Protocol approved May 2009.)

---

address a defined question to provide focus, direction, and an articulation of details about the potential resources needed to carry out the review. Consistent with the tenets of evidence-based practice, questions are understood to be emergent from the research context and can be

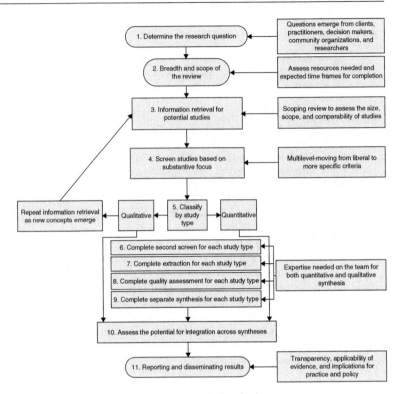

Figure 5.2 Steps for Conducting a Systematic Synthesis.

generated by clients, practitioners, decision makers, community organizations, researchers, and others interested in better understanding the practice or policy context. At minimum, a review question should address the target population and an intervention or phenomenon relevant to the practice or the policy field. The components of the question will help to determine what types of studies (quantitative, qualitative, or both) will be searched to provide the relevant information necessary for generating answers to the question. Systematic reviews are advantageous for answering questions, but only when used for the right questions (Dixon-Woods, Bonas, et al., 2006).

In our FGDM example, we had two questions we wanted to explore. The first question was whether FGDM is effective in terms of child safety, permanence of child's living situation, child and family well-being, and client satisfaction with the decision-making process. Because this was a question about effectiveness, we expected our systematic review would include intervention studies (e.g., randomized controlled trials, quasi-experimental designs) to assess whether the intervention worked as intended. Our second question was to explore the experiences of FGDM participants—for example, children, parents, workers, managers—involved in the intervention. Given that this question addressed the nature of client/professional perceptions about the intervention, qualitative studies were included in the overall review.

Step 2: Determine Breadth and Scope of the Review

Undertaking a systematic review for a social intervention can take a great deal of time and resources. Many reviews take as long as 2 years, though this may also be a function of limited funding and other resources. Users of research and evaluation evidence often need information more quickly. In collaboration with service users, reviewers should consider the breadth and scope of the project in order to determine resources needed to conduct the review and the expected time frames for completion. Decisions need to be made, however, if time and/or resources do not allow for a complete comprehensive review. In these cases, reviewers may need to compromise on the depth of the information retrieval strategy by limiting the scope of the review to include only provisional knowledge about a subject rather than proceeding with a full systematic review. Moreover, they may choose to embrace provisional methods developed to provide a systematic structure to identify different types studies in the literature that are nonetheless based on the principles of systematic reviews (Davies, 2003) but without the comprehensive and exhaustive designs for information retrieval. Examples of these methods include rapid evidence assessments and scoping reviews.

Rapid evidence assessment provides a systematic method for identifying relevant existing studies and facilitates comparisons between strands of evidence (Davies, 2003). The purpose of a rapid evidence assessment is to provide a systematic and transparent way of accumulating a sense of the current state of the research literature. Developed specifically for use in public policy research and evaluation (although its method is transferable to other practice and research contexts) a rapid evidence assessment is designed to search the electronic and print literature as comprehensively as possible within the constraints of a policy or practice timetable, collate descriptive outlines of the available evidence on a topic, critically appraise the evidence, sift out studies of poor quality, and provide an overview of what the evidence is saying (Davies, 2003).

Scoping reviews follow many of the same methodological steps as a systematic review (Dixon-Woods, Agarwal, Jones, Young, & Sutton, 2005; Kahn, Kunz, Kleijen, & Antle, 2003; Lavigne & Faier-Routman, 1993; Petticrew & Roberts, 2006), such as the use of rigorous and transparent methods for data collection, analysis, and interpretation (Glasziou, Irwin, Bain & Colditz, 2001; Weeks & Strudsholm, 2008). A key difference between scoping reviews and systematic reviews is that quality assessments are not typically included for scoping reviews due to differing conceptions of what *quality* means (Arksey, & O'Malley, 2005; Sandelowski, Docherty, & Emden, 1997). The main phases of a scoping review includes: (a) searching for relevant studies; (b) selected studies based on predetermined inclusion criteria; (c) extracting data; and(d) collating, summarizing, and reporting results. Although presented as a series of stages, the process is iterative, rather than linear, whereby steps may be repeated when needed to ensure the literature covered is comprehensive (Weeks & Strudsholm, 2008). Scoping reviews can provide a preliminary overview of the included results and can be an important first step in a qualitative synthesis because it can map out the evidence of the included studies. Scoping reviews can also provide the research team with a sense of the breadth of the evidence. By creating tables of retrieved evidence, the research team can learn about the included populations, sample strategies, methodologies, and data collection strategies used across the scoped studies.

In our FGDM example, we assembled a team of content and methods experts (in both quantitative and qualitative designs). Although there is an urgent need to determine whether FGDM works to keep children safe due to its widespread use and support and investment in its practice, it was important for the team to follow the methods for conducting systematic reviews to ensure the results were based on a comprehensive, exhaustive, and transparent review process. The team undertook in-depth quantitative analysis of outcomes of effectiveness and qualitative synthesis of the experiences of participants involved in FGDM, including children, parents, workers, and FGDM coordinators involved in delivering the intervention.

Step 3: Complete Information Retrieval Searches for Potential Studies

Systematic review procedures for information retrieval across methods for knowledge synthesis, including qualitative syntheses, must be comprehensive, transparent, and should include a variety of sources, published and unpublished. When locating qualitative studies, special attention may be necessary to draw creatively on literature that does not fit precise search criteria (Shaw, Booth, et al., 2004) to complement or add to a comprehensive search strategy. Although there is an ongoing debate about the need for comprehensive searches, we propose that the term *systematic* is used to emphasize a clearly specified, transparent, and comprehensive approach to literature searching. Explicit methods for searching are advantageous because they leave a trail for others to follow, they can be easily updated over the years, and they give the reader an indication of the biases that may be present in the inclusion or exclusion of certain studies. If a qualitative synthesis produces a large sample of primary studies, it may be possible to purposively sample from the larger collection of studies based on some explicit selection process. But we propose that sampling from primary studies without first considering the breadth of the evidence makes it difficult, if not impossible, to situate the sampled studies from the larger context of available evidence for a given research question. In other words, it defeats the purpose of a "systematic" synthesis, and there are no known methodologically sound ways of sampling that do not introduce the threat of substantial bias.

In our FGDM example, we first used a comprehensive information-retrieval strategy to locate both quantitative and qualitative results. We then complemented this search strategy by conducting "berry-picking" (Sandelowski & Barroso, 2007, p. 41), including footnote chasing, gray literature searches, author searching, hand searching selected journals, reference checking, and Google searching using qualitative methodology oriented locaters for evidence searching MOLES. Sandelowski and Barroso (2007) describe berry-picking as a dynamic and iterative process of searching for fugitive articles that are difficult to locate by modifying search terms and shifting searching strategies to uncover new articles that may be relevant to the study. Because berry-picking is done within the context of a systematic review, it is important to document all steps taken and record the variation of information retrieval strategies used within the search.

Step 4: Screen Based on the Substantive Focus of the Question

Screening of potentially relevant studies is completed by a minimum of two team members who review titles and abstracts based on agreed criteria for the inclusion of relevant studies. Compared to traditional literature reviews, a systematic synthesis provides an explicit and transparent set of criteria for including and excluding studies. Predeveloped inclusion and exclusion criteria are in line with the requirement of transparency of systematic reviews. To the degree that these can be clearly articulated, explicit criteria also facilitate more efficient and reliable screening of studies and extraction of data.

Rather than developing strict screening criteria at the outset, which can result in missed studies that are relevant to the question at hand, we propose that a proper screening process is multileveled, moving from liberal to more specific criteria based on the purposes of the review. At the first level of screening, the criteria should be based on the substantive focus of the question and not the design of the study. It has been our experience in screening titles and abstracts that abstracts often provide limited, incomplete, and insufficient details to make good decisions about inclusion based on methodological requirements. For example, screening for potential studies for the FGDM project was initially based on whether the article addressed FGDM, whether the article included a child-protection sample, and whether the article was a study (quantitative, qualitative, or both). By not placing restrictions on the type of study (just that it was a study), we were able to get a good sense of the different types of studies that have addressed FGDM in the literature.

Step 5: Classify by Study Type

Similar to the EPPI approach (Harden & Thomas, 2005) discussed in chapter 3, we propose that quantitative and qualitative studies should be separated and managed differently once all known studies have been located on the topic and the potential articles have been screened for relevance with respect to the substantive topic of the review. In a systematic review conducted by Saini and Léveillé (2011) to determine the effectiveness of research–practitioner collaboration and the experiences of stakeholders involved in these collaborations, no quantitative studies were found that addressed the research question. This was an important finding given the growing emphasis on the development of research–practitioner collaborations. Had we only searched for quantitative studies, we would have had an empty review. On the other hand, if we had only looked for qualitative studies, we could not have made such a strong statement about the state of the evidence. Based, then, on the synthesis of 21 qualitative studies exploring research and community collaborations, several elements that seemed to guide workable collaborations were reported, including embracing ambiguity within the collaboration, the reciprocal benefits of team membership, the balance between strong leadership and a cooperative process in which members willingly participate and share in planning and decision making, and meaningful involvement by sharing in both responsibilities and planning activities.

Step 6: Complete Separate Second Screen for Each Study Type

For quantitative studies of effectiveness, it is likely that further screening will be required due to the inclusion of different study designs (e.g., randomized controlled trials, quasi-experimental, cross-sectional, longitudinal) and the rigor of their designs (e.g., use of a control group, other potential sources of bias). In contrast, because there are no existing standard guidelines for screening out qualitative studies based on design, we argue that it is important that reviewers of qualitative research appreciate the epistemological and ontological differences inherent in qualitative approaches, because these may come to bear on the findings. Thus, knowledge of the different forms of qualitative research and their various strengths and weaknesses are paramount. Rather than excluding studies based on flaws in the study designs (e.g., small sample, limited reporting of procedures), reasons for exclusion should be based on the theoretical sensitivity of studies to the overall aims of the qualitative synthesis.

Step 7: Complete Separate Extraction for Each Study Type

Given the variability in qualitative designs and that extraction is often seen as an iterative process, there are very few extraction templates available as general guidelines. Deciding what data to extract will be influenced by the method chosen for completing the qualitative synthesis. For example, as introduced in chapter 2, some methods focus on aggregating the findings (e.g., meta-summary, content analysis), to determine the frequency of themes across studies. By using an aggregative method of analysis, data extraction includes documenting themes found in the findings, counting the number of times themes are found in the findings, and then demonstrating overall frequencies for each theme (Sandelowski & Barroso, 2007). In contrast, interpretive integrative techniques (e.g., meta-synthesis) provide interpretations of themes across studies by integrating findings from all studies where findings are reframed to create a new understanding of an event or phenomena (Sandelowski & Barroso, 2007). Although aggregative and integrative approaches contrast in their methods of synthesis, both focus primarily on the findings of the included studies and so data extraction is mainly focused on organizing, sifting, and sorting data from the findings sections of the original reports. Other more interpretive methods focus not only on the findings of the primary studies, but also on the different qualitative methods and theories in the original reports (e.g., meta-study, meta-ethnography). Distinctive to these methods, data extraction includes the mining of the entire research report not just the findings section. By explicitly following a method for qualitative synthesis, reviewers need to be cognizant of the specific ontological and epistemological frameworks, as well as the objectives, purposes, data collection techniques, and analytic approaches of their chosen method in order to remain consistent with their chosen method of synthesis.

Although data extraction is shaped by the chosen method, reviewers can still benefit from using qualitative software programs to help organize, sort, and sift the data according to the chosen method. Computer-assisted qualitative data analysis software (CAQDAS) allows for compact storage of data, saving and storage of each iteration of the data analysis, sharing of data with colleagues at a distance, hyperlinks for nonlinear organization of the data, tagging passages of text data, quickly coding passages for all documents, multiple coding for passages, a wide range of text search features, filtering data into sets or groupings, creating and storing memos and notes, and creating visual network maps to display relationships among selected components of the project (Drisko, 2004).

However, there are limitations of using CAQDAS programs. Designed to manage and organize data, they simply do not replace the primary role of the researcher as "analytic decision maker" (Drisko, 2004, p. 201). Further, Seidal (1991) argues that researchers, through the use of CAQDAS, can distance themselves from the raw data. Others note that CAQDAS can "push" the researcher toward a homogenization of analytical methods (Coffey, Holbrook, & Atkinson, 1996), or they may promote a "variable-oriented" approach to data analysis because researchers may move too quickly to building codes in the data rather than spending the needed time to sift through the data (Mason, 1996).

Being mindful of these limitations, we suggest that most CAQDAS are flexible enough to accommodate various methods for data extraction (e.g., NVivo 9.0, QSR International, Melbourne, Australia; Atlas.ti, Atlas.ti Scientific Software Development, Berlin, Germany; MAXQDA 10, VERBI, Marburg, Germany) and each may provide qualitative reviewers with the option of remaining iterative while providing some structure in data maintenance and organization. The main functions of computer packages include coding text, identifying key phrases, content analysis, and retrieval of coded sections of text. NVivo 9.0, Atlas.ti, and MAXQDA 10 now allow for pdf format to be imported into the programs, which greatly facilitates the inclusion of primary studies within systematic reviews.

Step 8: Complete Separate Quality Assessment for each Study Type

Given the range of quality of qualitative studies, reviewers will need to complete some form of quality assessment to assess the credibility, relevance, and applicability to the review. There are a number of examples of assessment forms that have been developed, but there remains a great deal of discrepancy with regard to how well these tools work. Many do not include distinctions between the different ontological and epistemological approaches, and standards for rigor, credibility, and relevance vary widely. Moreover, given the different philosophical assumptions of qualitative methods and the diversity of qualitative methods, universal criteria for judging quality have been challenged. Our more pragmatic approach incorporates a broad-based tool for assessing quality. We strongly believe that, if the research question dictates the design of the study, then questions of quality should adhere to the procedures of the method chosen. In chapter 6, we present a quality appraisal tool that has been developed to accommodate various qualitative methods and prompts reviewers to systematically ascertain whether the study is of high quality on a number of dimensions. Although there is no consensus about what would constitute a "good enough" appraisal tool for qualitative research, we contend that reviewers nevertheless need to find ways to assess quality in order to weight the contribution of any single study. Thus, regardless of which appraisal form is used to assess quality, and whether readers choose to adopt our tool, reviewers need to be explicit about their rationale and process for assessing quality, and how this process becomes included in the overall integration of primary studies. After all, though there may not be agreement on how to assess quality, most can surely agree that there are studies within the literature that are of varying quality.

Step 9: Complete Separate Synthesis for Each Study Type

Once studies have been screened for relevancy, assessed for quality, and extracted, the more formal process of synthesis begins. Although the reviewer is continuously considering the synthesis of data throughout the project, it is helpful to think of the synthesis as a unique step in the review process given the complexity and intricacy involved in making sense of the grouping of studies for the review. Qualitative synthesis is distinguished from quantitative synthesis (e.g., meta-analysis) because of its focus on the interpretive integration of qualitative data to explore events, concepts, or phenomena (e.g., phenomenologies, ethnographies, grounded theories, and other descriptions of phenomena).

What to synthesize and how to go about doing this will depend on the question(s) being asked and on the method chosen for qualitative synthesis. For example, aggregative methods may include an empirical approach for synthesis where findings are abstracted into themes and subthemes to uncover common elements and content. Integrative approaches may keep the original meaning of the primary studies while deconstructing and reconstructing findings in order to develop new interpretations. Indeed, these integrations offer more than the sum of their individual data points because they provide new interpretations (Bertero & Chamberlain Wilmoth, 2007). Interpretive synthesis may include discursive strategies to consider differences, patterns, and methodological inconsistencies leading to the creation of new conceptualization of the event or phenomena. Again, we emphasize that in this review stage, researchers should be aware of the overall purpose, objectives, and epistemological frameworks of methods of individual studies that they are synthesizing, as well as the method chosen for the review.

Step 10: Assess The Potential for Integration Across Syntheses and Synthesizing Where Possible

As both quantitative and qualitative studies are separately synthesized, reviewers may question whether there would be any merit of integrating these two groups of studies into a mixed-method design. Although Bayesian meta-analysis and realist synthesis are emerging strategies for combining qualitative and quantitative methods (as reviewed in chapter 3), there are benefits to completing separate analysis of qualitative and quantitative studies. In the systematic review approach of conducting separate synthesis of quantitative and qualitative studies, each synthesis can enhance the applicability and relevance of the other. Consistent with enhancement model, developed by Popay (2006), of integrating qualitative research into systematic reviews, conducting separate analyses of qualitative and quantitative syntheses allows for consideration of both types of evidence. This may be a unique and important contribution to knowledge development that might also provide the opportunity to assess the compatibility and differences of findings based on the two different methods for analysis.

Within this enhancement model, qualitative synthesis can contribute to systematic reviews at various stages within the review process (see Figure 5.3).

In the beginning phase of the systematic review, qualitative synthesis can provide information about the contextual factors to consider in developing the systematic review protocol, including issues related to the theory of change, choice of outcomes to be used in the analysis, choosing moderator variables, and finding issues relevant to implementation. In the middle phase of the systematic review, qualitative synthesis can enhance a meta-analysis by providing important information about

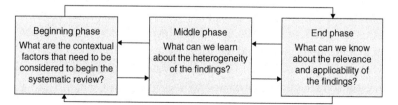

Figure 5.3 Phases of Integrating Qualitative Synthesis Within Systematic Reviews.

the influences of heterogeneity in the findings. For example, qualitative synthesis can provide critical information about the influence of different recruitment procedures, levels of adherence to the intervention, issues regarding dosage, the experience of participants within the interventions, and the role of facilitators. In the FGDM review, separating qualitative and quantitative analysis provides the opportunity to first explore overall effect sizes based on quantitative results of effectiveness and then to integrate these findings with the experiences shared by those involved in the intervention. If the effect sizes seem high or low, the perspectives of the participants may shed new understanding on why the intervention worked or did not work. At the end phase, qualitative synthesis can be used to explore the relevancy and applicability of findings to local contexts. At this stage, additional evidence should be searched to locate new evidence not previously included. Special attention here is on finding different perspectives and experiences (e.g., negative cases). A more complete understanding of the current evidence provides clarity in discussing the transferability of results to other populations and making exploratory links to the overall applicability of the findings to populations not included in the study samples used for the systematic review.

Using the FGDM review as an example, the meta-analysis of the quantitative studies found no significant difference of maltreatment recurrences. However, families receiving FGDM tended to receive more services and expressed greater satisfaction with these services than families receiving usual care. Therefore, had we limited the systematic review to quantitative studies, it would have precluded inclusion of qualitative studies that can provide information regarding other types of benefits that FGDM may have for regarding child/family well-being and satisfaction with service delivery.

Including qualitative studies offered additional clarity regarding recurrence, placement stability, and services. Moreover, qualitative questions provided greater insight into the transitional phases of FGDM (see Figure 5.4), such as the implementation of the intervention, the process of the intervention, and the relevance and applicability of the intervention across jurisdictions. The implementation strategies covered issues regarding recruitment strategies, demographics considerations (e.g., culture, language, socioeconomic issues), and service resourcing (e.g., staffing issues, qualifications, supervision, and training). The process of the

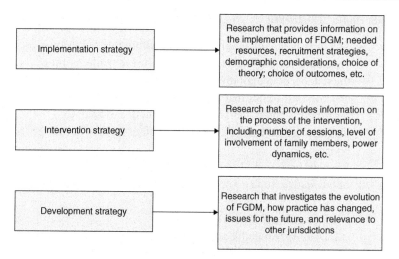

Figure 5.4   The Strategic Framework and the Development of the Research Projects. Adapted from the American Humane Association, 2005.

intervention included any discrepancies in the implementation of the intervention from the program theory, the perceived involvement of families, the method for facilitating meetings, and ways in which cultural issues were addressed. The development strategy included whether decisions were supported by all parties, the quality of plans, the experiences of participants, and policy- and practice-related issues.

Step 11: Dissemination of Results

There are various ways of disseminating systematic review results using different formats and for different audiences: full reports, brief reports, one-page summaries, for example. Careful consideration must be made to contextualize findings and to weigh their applicability and potential transferability to other populations. The question is whether knowledge gained from qualitative studies should remain local or whether the knowledge should be transferred and integrated across studies, which will influence one's attitude about the appropriateness of synthesis of qualitative findings. In other words, the question is not whether to do research but whether it applies beyond the population studied.

KEY POINTS TO REMEMBER

- The inclusion of qualitative synthesis within the "family of systematic reviews" helps to move qualitative synthesis out of the shadow of quantitative synthesis; provides impetus to the creation of methods that are transparent, consistent, and rigorous regardless of the systematic review method; and helps to distinguish qualitative synthesis from other types of narrative reviews.
- We have proposed 11 steps for conducting systematic synthesis of qualitative studies:

  1. Determine the research question.
  2. Determine breadth and scope of the review.
  3. Complete information retrieval searches for potential studies.
  4. Screen based on the substantive focus of the question.
  5. Classify by study type.
  6. Complete separate second screen for each study type.
  7. Complete separate extraction for each study type.
  8. Complete separate quality assessment for each study type.
  9. Complete separate synthesis for each study type.
  10. Assess the potential for integration across syntheses.
  11. Dissemination of results.

SUGGESTED READING

Arksey, H., & O'Malley, L. (2005). Scoping studies: Towards a methodological framework. *International Journal of Social Research Methodology, 8*(1), 19–32.

Dixon-Woods, M., & Fitzpatrick, R. (2001). Qualitative research in systematic reviews. *BMJ, 323,* 65–66.

Dixon-Woods, M., Bonas, S., Booth, A., Jones, D. R., Miller, T., Sutton, A. J., . . . Young, B. (2006). How can systematic reviews incorporate qualitative research? A critical perspective. *Qualitative Research, 6,* 27–44.

Dixon-Woods, M., Fitzpatrick, R., & Roberts, K. (2001). Including qualitative research in systematic reviews: Opportunities and problems. *Journal of Evaluation in Clinical Practice, 7*(2), 125–133.

Jensen, L., & Allen, M. (1996). Meta-synthesis of qualitative findings. *Qualitative Health Research, 6,* 553–560.

Pope, C., Mays, N., & Popay, J. (2007). *Synthesizing qualitative and quantitative health research: A guide to methods.* Berkshire, U.K.: Open University Press.

Schreiber, R., Crooks, D., & Stern, P. (1997). Qualitative meta-analysis. In J. Morse (Ed.), *Completing a qualitative project: Details and dialogue.* Thousand Oaks, CA: Sage.

Sherwood, G. (1999). Meta-synthesis: Merging qualitative studies to develop nursing knowledge. *International Journal for Human Caring, 3,* 32–42.

Thomas, J., Harden, A. Oakley, A., Oliver, S., Sutcliffe, K., Rees, R., . . . Kavanagh, J. (2004). Integrating qualitative research with trials in systematic reviews. *BMJ, 328*(7446), 1010–1012.

Walsh, D., & Downe, S. (2005). Meta-synthesis method for qualitative research: A literature review. *Journal of Advanced Nursing, 50*(2), 204–211.

6

Searching and Screening Qualitative Studies

LITERATURE REVIEWS IN QUALITATIVE RESEARCH: FRAMING THE DEBATE

By way of introduction to this chapter, we first make note of some of the debates and tensions among scholars regarding the utility of even conducting a literature review within a qualitative research endeavor. This sets the stage for considering where systematic reviews fit within the space of this debate, allows us to review the unique and essential features of a systematic review, and, in a more sustained way, fleshes out the various strategies of searching for qualitative research within systematic reviews.

The current terrain of qualitative research is marked by a lack of consensus among its scholars on the value of literature reviews, the best manner in which to conduct and include other literature, and the amount of weight to be given to prior literature within the qualitative inquiry process. Some qualitative researchers propose that a literature review should be set aside in primary research until after the data collection process so as not to distort the emerging discovery of concepts, themes, and theories (Glaser, 1978). This notion of "ignorance is bliss" (Shank, 2002) contends that conducting literature searches in the initial phases of research limits the free flow of ideas and can unduly influence or obfuscate the emergent nature of qualitative research designed to explore the context-sensitive experiences of the participants (Johnson & Christensen, 2008). For those researchers favoring a literature review, reviews are understood to help frame the research process and can assist in informing the researcher about various contextualized influences that might iteratively shape the data collection process and findings. Moreover, they have the potential of providing texture to the settings, situations, and populations included in the study (Strauss & Corbin, 1990). Padgett (1998) further offers that literature reviews shape the study, providing prior context to the research, and, importantly, promote the advance of knowledge by building on other studies.

In a similar vein to those propounding the practice of extensive literature review, systematic reviews are grounded in the assumption that knowledge accumulates and that people learn from, and build on, what others have done (Neuman, 2003). Likewise, Cooper and Hedges (1994) have noted that the literature review is prized by scholars and practitioners because it serves a strategic function in managing information overload and facilitating access to the extant knowledge in a particular area of inquiry. However, as we have taken considerable time to point out, systematic reviews differ from other conventional literature review practices because they insist on the inclusion of all relevant studies, without regard for one's personal favorites or the consideration of the results found. Moreover, systematic reviews are explicitly inclusive, transparent, and specific with respect to inclusion and exclusion criteria, a set of practices that further distinguish systematic reviews from other reviewing processes. We develop these themes in the following sections.

Given the lack of consensus about the utility of literature reviews, it is not surprising that there are divergent views on ways to search the literature and what to include when conducting systematic synthesis. Although there has been progress in developing methods to include qualitative research within evidence-based practice and systematic reviews, information retrieval for qualitative studies remains one of the least developed areas in systematic review methods (Dixon-Woods, Bonas, et al., 2006; Flemming & Briggs, 2007).

CONSIDERATIONS FOR SYSTEMATIC LITERATURE REVIEWS

Iterative Versus Comprehensive Searches for Qualitative Synthesis

Some scholars contend that purposive sampling techniques are more consistent with qualitative methods because they focus on purposive sampling strategies (Dixon-Woods et al., 2006), a position more aligned with the iterative process within qualitative inquiry. Doyle (2003) states that, "like meta-analysis, meta-ethnography [a method of qualitative synthesis] utilizes multiple empirical studies but, unlike meta-analysis, the sample is purposive rather than exhaustive because the purpose is interpretive explanation and not prediction" (p. 326). However, this argument can be made for all forms of qualitative inquiry (that is, none are predictive endeavors). Others have suggested using sampling strategies developed for primary qualitative methods, such as searching the literature until reaching "theoretical saturation" based on emerging themes (Paterson, Thorne, & Dewis, 1998; Schreiber, Crooks, & Stern, 1997) or seeking negative cases to aim for maximum heterogeneity (Dixon-Woods, Bonas, et al., 2006). Supporters of purposive sampling techniques for information retrieval argue that these methods remain faithful to the iterative process in primary qualitative studies.

On the other hand, supporters of systematic synthesis endorse comprehensive searches to retrieve qualitative studies for systematic reviews and argue that inclusive approaches to searching improve the overall quality of the review (Booth, 2006). The idea is to retrieve all potentially relevant studies in order to create a larger interpretive understanding of the studies examined to answer a specified research question (Barroso et al., 2003). Similar to comprehensive searches for RCTs for meta-analytic purposes (Cooper, 1998), systematic information retrieval strategies of qualitative studies include sufficiently exhaustive searches, an "interest in synthesizing empirical studies" (Noblit & Hare, 1988, p. 10), and transparent approaches for the inclusion and integration or interpretation of studies (Barroso et al., 2003). Whereas the primary purpose of meta-analysis is "pooling data across studies" (Littell, Corcoran, & Pillai, 2008, p. 79), qualitative methods for synthesis often remain faithful to the interpretative nature of qualitative inquiry, once all potential studies are included in the analysis. Dixon-Woods et al. (2006) argue this point but also seem to warn reviewers to hold close the basic tenets of systematic reviews, stating:

> It could be argued that once systematic reviews fail to be explicit and reproducible, and allowed to include (apparently) idiosyncratically chosen literatures and to use non-transparent forms of interpretation to determine synthesis of the included studies, they are no longer

systematic. In fact, it could be asserted, reviews of this type are nothing new: they are simply literature reviews of the type that have always been done (p. 37).

Systematic information retrieval strategies of qualitative studies are a "distinctive enterprise" (Sandelowski & Barroso, 2007, p. 22) and stand in contrast to traditional literature reviews or theoretical selections of studies. The aim of systematic information retrieval of qualitative studies is to use the research question as a basis for developing approaches designed to optimally search for all potentially relevant articles and to exclude irrelevant articles (Shaw et al., 2004). Search strategies include published and unpublished primary information, and finds from this process are then digested, sifted, classified, simplified, and synthesized (Manten, 1973).

From our standpoint, both literature reviews and systematic reviews have their place, but a literature review should not be called systematic unless it incorporates the following criteria as outlined within the family of systematic reviews:

1. The information retrieval strategy includes a comprehensive process for retrieval of all studies relevant to the research question of the review (studies may include qualitative, quantitative, or mixed-methods depending on the research question).
2. There is transparency with respect to the decisions made in searching for potential studies (list of key terms used, keyword searching strategies used, decisions regarding years covered, cultural context and geographical locations included/excluded), and the level of detail is sufficient for replication.
3. Both published and unpublished studies are included in the search and inclusion of relevant studies.
4. Multiple sources are used to retrieve potentially relevant studies (e.g., electronic databases, personal contacts, reference checking, hand searches of journals, gray literature searches).

Challenges for Locating Qualitative Research Articles

For qualitative research to be included in systematic reviews, reviewers must be able to retrieve studies easily and efficiently (Wilczynski & Haynes, 2002). However, there are a number of challenges for locating qualitative studies, which we outline herein, including the variability of qualitative methods, the spread of qualitative studies across journals, nonspecific qualitative titles and abstracts, deficiencies in bibliographic indexes, lack of expertise in locating qualitative research, and the lack of evidence about the best ways to locate qualitative research. Because of the scope of these challenges, however, information retrieval is resource-intensive (Sandelowski & Barroso, 2007). Careful consideration of the resources needed, including time for information retrieval, should thus be made before a review is initiated.

The Variability of Qualitative Methods

Qualitative research encompasses a variety of methods and approaches (including, ethnography, phenomenology, grounded theory, and discourse analysis), which leads to inconsistencies in the naming of qualitative research (Evans, 2002). Locating studies across various qualitative methods is further limited based on which database is searched. Social Work Abstracts database, for example, does not adequately index qualitative terms. Similar issues have been noted in MEDLINE and PsychInfo, as they each use fewer indexed terms regarding qualitative methodologies (e.g., ethnography, phenomenology, grounded theory, and discourse analysis) and instead use more general descriptions of qualitative research (e.g., qualitative, interviews) (Wilczynski, Marks, Haynes, 2007). CINAHL, on the other hand, is a database geared toward nursing and allied health professions, and it has been found to have a larger number of qualitative methodology terms (Evans, 2002).

Qualitative Studies Spread Across Journals

Qualitative research has been embraced by various fields, including social work, nursing, medicine, politics, law, psychology, anthropology, and sociology. Thus, qualitative research that might bear on key questions in the field of social work can be found across a multitude of journals spanning many disciplines (McKibbon & Gadd, 2006).

Nonspecific Titles and Abstracts

Qualitative titles and abstracts often focus on the content of the findings and not necessarily the methods used in the studies (Evans, 2002; McKibbon, Wilczynski, & Haynes, 2006). Therefore, traditional information retrieval methods that focus on locating studies by using search terms found within titles and abstracts are generally not adequate for locating qualitative studies (McKibbon et al., 2006). Although descriptive findings can provide a rich context for conducting studies, this also adds to the complexity of database searches in identifying qualitative research on specific questions (Evans, 2002). In addition, authors of primary studies and reviewers conducting systematic reviews may differ in how they define concepts located in titles and abstracts, which can contribute to failed database searches (Lowe & Barnett, 1994). Searches that are too broad to capture the variations of reporting by primary authors may result in the retrieval of many thousands of irrelevant papers. Although this does not necessarily reflect on the quality of the research, it increases the difficulty of finding these studies. As Flemming and Briggs (2007) point out, proper indexes depend on authors providing sufficient detail about methods used.

Deficiencies in Bibliographic Indexes

The development of bibliographic database indexing systems for qualitative designs has not kept pace with the field's indexing of quantitative designs (Evans, 2002). Therefore, searching for qualitative studies is limited by the deficiencies of electronic database indexing, as these often do not adequately capture the variability of methods used in qualitative research (Walters, Wilczynski, & Haynes, 2006).

Lack of Expertise in Locating Qualitative Research

Although many librarians involved in information retrieval for systematic reviews are proficient at locating RCTs, quasi-experimental designs, and other intervention-based studies (Wade, Turner, Rothstein, & Lavenberg, 2006), less is known about the optimal ways to locate qualitative studies from these same databases (Wilczynski et al., 2007), making qualitative research a more difficult and challenging enterprise (Dixon-Woods & Fitzpatrick, 2001).

Lack of Evidence About the Best Ways to Locate Qualitative Research

There is little research on the specificity and sensitivity of indexing for qualitative research (Evans, 2002). There are emerging strategies for searching for qualitative studies, but few have been empirically tested and little is known about the sensitivity and specificity of different search strategies across different electronic databases (Shaw et al., 2004). The risk is that potentially relevant qualitative studies may be missed during the information retrieval process (Evans, 2002).

Strategies for Systematic Information Retrieval of Qualitative Studies

Developing Relevant Search Terms

Developing an electronic search strategy begins with an iterative process of finding and assessing the best ways to search electronic databases and to modify searches based on what has already been retrieved. For example, a systematic review of the prevention of cyber abuse targeting children and adolescents (Mishna, Cook, Saini, Wu, & McFadden, 2011) found no studies to be included in their review when searching for "cyber abuse." However, based on a brief search of terms used for prevention programs with this targeted group, it was uncovered that these interventions were addressing "cyber safety." Prior to conducting a systematic review, mapping the terms can be helpful for further refining the question, establishing relevance, and choosing the best search terms. Some terms may also have different meanings, depending on geographical location. For example, topics covering child abuse or child maltreatment can also be located using regional terms, such as "child welfare," "child protection," and "social care." Developing a clear question based on the population parameters, context, and locations can help to develop a list of search terms that may be useful in locating studies relevant to the question.

Strategies for Electronic Databases

Because qualitative research is conducted by many disciplines, researchers will often need to locate studies contained in multiple, disciplinary-specific databases (see Table 6.1). For example, a research question exploring experiences of parenting in times of distress could be published in journals specific to the fields of social work, health, education, law, or sociology, for example. Careful attention is required to consider the various fields that may have explored a research question and to develop strategies for selecting electronic databases accordingly. Questions in the preparation of building efficient search strategies include: What are the key concepts to be searched? How are these represented in each discipline? What are their related terms? How are these key concepts represented in the controlled vocabulary within each database to be searched?

The Use of Controlled Vocabulary

The use of controlled vocabulary or indexing systems found within bibliographic databases (known as thesaurus terms or subject headings) has

Table 6.1 Sample Disciplinary Databases Across Professions

Electronic Database	Profession
Social Work Abstracts	Social work
CINAHL	Nursing
MEDLINE	Medicine and health sciences
PsychInfo	Psychology
Sociological Abstracts	Sociology
ERIC	Education
Criminal Justice Abstracts	Law
ASSIA	Applied social sciences
Ageline	Gerontology and geriatrics

received some attention in the current ways of locating qualitative research (Evans, 2002), but indexes in qualitative research are not as developed as their quantitative counterparts (Barroso, Sandelowski, & Voils, 2006). The thesaurus terms used in each database vary according to their specific indexing system. For example, qualitative research is indexed on PsychInfo as "qualitative research" with related terms including "grounded theory" and "interviews" and "observation methods." On ERIC, their subject indexing of "qualitative research" has more detailed related terms, including "case studies," "ethnography," "field studies," "naturalist observation," and "transcripts (written record)." On MEDLINE, the only option for indexing is to use the term "qualitative research," whereas in Social Work Abstracts, indexing for qualitative research is not available.

The Use of Free-Text Filters

Free-text terms, or "raw text," can identify qualitative research terms by searching for these words within titles, abstracts, and keywords of articles within the various databases. Free-text filters are preformulated search strategies that have been developed by librarians to help retrieve articles in databases that deal with qualitative research. Examples of free-text combinations for qualitative research are presented in Boxes 6.1 and 6.2. These filters commonly use terms to describe qualitative methods (e.g., "grounded theory," "ethnography," or "phenomenological") and data collection methods relevant to qualitative research (e.g., "interviews," "purposive sampling," "focus groups," or "observations"). However, given that many qualitative studies do not specify methods or data collection designs

---

Box 6.1   Example of a Free-Text Filter for Qualitative Research for MEDLINE

Ovid Medline

(qualitative [tw] OR ethnolog* [tw] OR ethnog* [tw] OR ethnomethodolog* [tw] OR emic [tw] OR etic[tw] OR phenomenolog*[tw]) OR (hermeneutic* [tw] OR participant observ* [tw] OR constant compar* [tw]) OR (focus group* [tw] OR grounded theory [tw] OR narrative analysis [tw] OR lived experience* [tw] OR life experience* [tw]) OR (maximum variation [tw] OR snowball [tw]) OR (theoretical sample* [tw] OR theoretical sampling [tw] OR purposive sample* [tw] OR purposive sampling [tw] OR (Nursing Methodology Research [mesh]) OR (metasynthes* [tw] OR meta-synthes* [tw] OR metasummar* [tw] OR metastudy [tw] OR metastudies [tw] OR meta-study [tw] OR meta-studies [tw]) OR (tape recording OR "tape record*" [tw] OR "video record*" [tw] OR taperecord* [tw] OR audiorecord* [tw] OR videotap* [tw] OR videorecord*[tw] or "action research" [tw])

*tw = title word.

---

within titles and abstracts, it is difficult to assess the sensitivity of these filters to capture all the relevant qualitative studies for a review question. In the MEDLINE search (box 6.1), for example, each of the "tw" or title word searches are separated by OR rather than AND in order to capture

---

Box 6.2   Example of a Free-Text Filter for Qualitative Research for PsychInfo

CSA PsychInfo

(qualitative OR ethnol* OR ethnog* OR ethnonurs* OR emic OR etic OR field note* OR field record* OR fieldnote* OR field stud* participant observ* OR participant observation* OR hermaneutic* OR phenomenolog* OR lived experience* OR grounded theory OR constant compar* OR theoretical sampl* OR content analy* OR thematic analy* OR narrative* OR unstructured categor* OR structured categor* OR unstructured interview* OR semi-structured interview* OR maximum variation* OR snowball OR audio* OR tape* OR video* OR metasynthes* OR meta-synthes* OR metasummar* OR meta-summar* OR metastud* OR meta-stud* OR meta-ethnograph* OR metaethnog* OR meta-narrative* OR metanarrat* OR meta-interpretation* OR metainterpret* OR qualitative meta-analy* OR qualitative metaanaly* OR qualitative meta analy* OR purposive sampl* OR action research OR focus group*)

Filters adapted from Linda Slater, Liaison Librarian, Faculty of Nursing and the Centre for Health Promotion Studies University of Alberta Libraries John W. Scott Health Sciences Library in 2008 (http://www.ualberta.ca/~lslater/QualFilters.html).

---

more terms rather than limit them. In addition, a truncation wildcard (*) is used for base terms that can have multiple meanings. Truncation instructs the database to return all words with the root term to the left of the wildcard. For instance, the term "ethnog*" will return articles using the words ethnography, ethnographic, ethnographer, ethnogrophers, and ethnographies, for example.

The Use of Broad-Based Terms

Broad-based terms or the choosing of common terms used in qualitative research such as "qualitative" or "interview*" can also be included within information-retrieval strategies. Flemming and Briggs (2007) report that simple search strategies using broad-based terms were as effective as complex ones (free text) in locating qualitative research examining patients' experiences of living with a leg ulcer.

The Need for a Comprehensive Approach for Searching Electronic Databases

Shaw et al. (2004), in their attempt to determine recall (potentially relevant records found) and precision (actual relevant records found), used six electronic databases to search for qualitative studies using indexing terms, free-text terms, and broad-based terms. Overall, they found that limiting their search strategy to one strategy (indexing terms, free-text terms, or broad-based terms) missed relevant hits. Indexing had the highest precision and broad-based searching had the highest recall. The investigators concluded that their findings confirm that all three strategies are likely to result in a large number of false positives and irrelevant hits. They further suggested that searching for qualitative research should not rely on a singular method, but should include a range of search strategies to increase the positive hits. Given the rather sparse empirical testing of indexing, filters, and broad-based searches for qualitative research, caution and, perhaps, liberal or inclusive search strategies are needed when developing searches for systematic reviews.

Searching Indexes for Study Design by Using Methodological Filters

Because many, if not most, electronic databases do not adequately index by study design, it is generally recommended to avoid searching with methodological filters (this applies for both quantitative and qualitative methods) until such methods for indexing by design improve and have been sufficiently tested for sensitivity (the flexibility of terms used to capture the maximum relevant studies) and specificity (the accuracy of terms used to locate relevant studies) (Wade et al., 2006).

Other Searching Strategies

Search strategies for systematic reviews commonly include other methods in addition to electronic searching (Figure 6.1), including footnote chasing, hand searching, consultation, and fugitive searching (Wade et al., 2006).

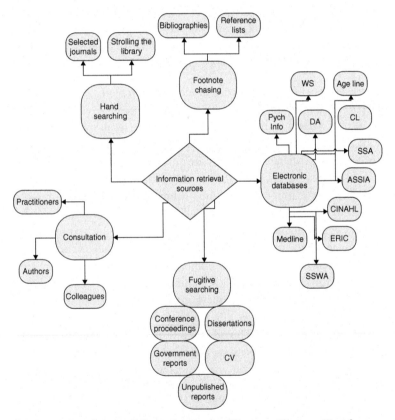

Figure 6.1 Comprehensive Information Retrieval Strategy. Please see Text for Database Explanations. CV = Curriculum Vitae, DA = Dissertation Abstracts, CL = Cochrane Library, SSA = Social Science Abstracts . Adapted from The Handbook of Research Synthesis, by H. Cooper and L. Hedges, 1994. Copyright 1994 by Sage Foundation.

These additional search methods are needed to locate studies that might have been missed by electronic searching. Despite the apparent utility of employing these strategies, Flemming and Briggs (2007) note that none of these methods have been adequately tested to determine whether they add additional value to information-retrieval procedures for qualitative studies.

Footnote Chasing

Reviewers should check the reference lists of all relevant articles that are obtained, including those from previously published reviews. Potentially relevant articles that are identified should be retrieved and assessed for possible inclusion in the review.

Consultation

Face-to-face discussions at meetings, e-mails, requests on Listservs, and formal letters of request for information from authors, presenters, and experts should be solicited to assist the review team to locate relevant studies. A list of the inclusion criteria for the review, along with a sample of relevant articles, should be sent to these key informants along with the request for additional studies.

Hand searching

Hand searching involves conducting manual searches of highly relevant journals to uncover potentially eligible studies that might have been missed through electronic searches. Potential studies might be missed by electronic database searching given that titles and abstracts are often insufficient for identifying eligible studies in quantitative systematic reviews (Higgins & Green, 2006; Littell et al., 2008), and this problem may be even worse for titles and abstracts of qualitative studies (Evans, 2002). Although no studies have compared the hits between electronic database searches and hand searching for qualitative research, Turner et al. (2003) found that electronic databases missed almost two-thirds of RCTs identified by hand searching.

Gray Literature Searches

Gray literature searches are also known as *fugitive literature* because they attempt to locate studies that are not normally found and are difficult to retrieve through conventional methods, such as electronic database searches. These can include conference proceedings, research reports, government reports, book chapters, dissertations, policy documents, and research organizations' Web sites. Special attention should be made to search and collect relevant studies captured in the gray literature. Locating gray literature is an important step in conducting systematic reviews (Wade et al., 2006) and the search for fugitive literature is one of the key distinguishing features of systematic reviews (both qualitative and quantitative) of search engines (e.g., Google) that can be performed for this task, but it is important to consult with a librarian to develop the necessary skills to sift through the many hits that are sure to result from such an endeavor. For examples of gray literature, see Box 6.3.

Screening for Relevant Studies

The screening of potentially relevant studies helps to assess which studies should be included in the review. A predeveloped set of inclusion criteria ensures transparency and helps guarantee the credibility of the screening process. During the systematic review process, an article must pass through various checkpoints to assess whether it should be included in the final review. Establishing clear checkpoints allows multiple reviewers (at least two) to score articles based on preexisting criteria, and these scores can be checked for interrater agreement at each stage. Although there are a variety of ways to screen for the inclusion of studies, we have found that using checkpoints of increasing scrutiny is the most efficient way to proceed. Although each systematic review will vary regarding the number of checkpoints needed during the review, we recommend that three general screening points should be a part of every review process: (a) initial screening, (b) strict screening, and (c) data extraction form.

Initial Screening (level 1)

The first stage consists of an initial screening to quickly determine whether a study might be appropriate for the review based on the study's title, abstract, and bibliographic information. Again, screening qualitative studies from titles and abstracts can be difficult because there is often insufficient information in the titles and abstracts to suggest the study design (Evans, 2002). The same, though, can be said for quantitative studies, and there is a growing interest in developing standard abstracts to include information about the study designs (Hartley, Sydes, & Blurton, 1996; McIntosh, 1994). Therefore, the purpose of this initial screening is to include all possible relevant studies related to the objectives of the systematic review and the inclusion and exclusion criteria. Given the problems of locating and screening studies based simply on abstracts, we suggest that

---

Box 6.3   Example of Select Gray Literature Web Sites

Gray Literature Web sites

- GreyNet Listserv: listserv@greynet.org
- GrayLIT: http://www.osti.gov/graylit/
- The Grey Literature Report: http://www.nyam.org/library/pages/grey_literature_report
- NHS Evidence: http://www.evidence.nhs.uk/
- System for Information on Grey Literature in Europe: http://opensigle.inist.fr/
- MedlinePlus: http://www.nlm.nih.gov/medlineplus/

Conference proceedings and abstracts

- PapersFirst: http://www.oclc.org/ca/en/global/default.htm
- NLM Gateway: http://gateway.nlm.nih.gov/gw/Cmd

Theses and dissertations

- British Library Electronic Theses Online Service: http://EThOS.bl.uk
- Networked Digital Library of Theses and Dissertations (NDLTD): http://www.theses.org/

Research Reports

- Research reports (http://www.evaluationcanada.ca/site.cgi?s=6&ss=8); Government reports and policy documents
- http://www.gc.ca/publications/publication-eng.html
- http://publications.gov.au/
- http://www.natlib.govt.nz/collections/types-of-items/government-publications
- http://europa.eu/index_en.htm

Synthesis organizations

- Centers for Disease Control and Prevention's (CDC) Guide to Community Preventative Services: www.thecommunityguide.org
- Database of Abstracts of Reviews of Effects (DARE): www.york.ac.uk/inst/crd/darehp.htm
- HTA Database: www.york.ac.uk/inst/crd/htahp.htm
- NHS Economic Evaluation Database (NEED): www.york.ac.uk/inst/crd/nhsdhp.htm
- Cochrane Collaboration: www.cochrane.org

- Campbell Collaboration (C2): www.campbellcollaboration.org
- Evidence for Policy and Practice Information and Co-ordinating Centre (EPPI-Centre): http://eppi.ioe.ac.uk
- Joanna Briggs Institute: http://www.joannabriggs.edu.au
- Centre for Public Health Excellence Nice (National Institute for Health and Clinical Evidence): www.publichealth.nice.org.uk
- New Zealand Health Technology Assessment (NZHTA): http://nzhta. chmeds.ac.nz/publications.htm#review

reviewers do not screen for study design, but that consideration should be made for study design once all potentially relevant studies relating to the substantive question are included and full text articles are retrieved. Questions appropriate at this first level of screening include:

1. Does this article describe a research study (e.g., contains a sample and is not a commentary, theory paper, program description)?
2. Is the population related to the purpose of the review?
3. Is the experience/phenomenon/intervention/prevention/tool related to the purpose of the review?

The two raters are trained to assess reliability on a small number of cases and to quickly review article titles and abstracts for inclusion on this small and easily discernible set of questions. Four outcomes for each screen are possible: both agree "no"; both agree "yes"; the raters disagree; or at least one of the raters is unsure. Both agree "yes," both agree "unsure," and disagreements should proceed to the level 2 screening. It is crucial, at each screening level, to save records and to document all decisions, including which studies were passed to the next screening level and which were dropped.

Strict Screening (level 2)

The second stage consists of a strict screening form where reviewers are given full copies of articles to determine whether studies should remain in the review. If the systematic review is considering a qualitative question, then specific questions will need to be developed to explore the types of methods that will be included in the review. If the research question includes both quantitative and qualitative designs, then this stage may be the most appropriate time to separate the results by whether the study is quantitative or qualitative (see Figure 6.2).

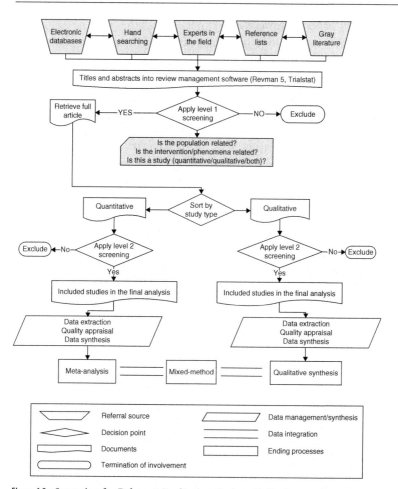

Figure 6.2. Screening for Relevant Studies in a Systematic Review.

Differences between coders should be identified and resolved to ensure consistent screening of the studies and to establish interrater reliability. Any discrepancies should be subsequently resolved by referral back to the source of the material and conflicts resolved by a third reviewer based on the original source. If vital information is missing from the original reports, reviewers should contact the corresponding author by e-mail in an attempt to retrieve the necessary data for the screening.

Data Extraction Form (level 3)

The third stage consists of a data extraction form to log data from the articles that have made it past the first two screenings. For reviews that include both quantitative and qualitative designs, reviewers will want to read Littell et al.'s (2008) pocket guide for systematic reviews and meta-analysis in which they provide a clear and descriptive process for formatting and developing the contents of data extraction forms for quantitative data to be used in meta-analysis. The strategies and methods for data extraction for qualitative analysis will depend on the method chosen for synthesizing the primary studies. Generally, data extraction of qualitative studies should include: (a) the source, (b) date of publication, (c) location of the study, (d) setting of the study, (e) purpose of study, (f) theoretical orientation, (g) sampling procedures, (h) sample size, (i) method for data collection, (j) methods for data analysis, (k) strengths of the study, (l) limitations of the study, and (m) major findings.

SEARCH STRATEGIES FOR STUDIES RELEVANT TO A SYSTEMATIC REVIEW—AN ILLUSTRATION

As an illustration of these strategies, we present an information-retrieval strategy that we conducted for all potential studies (both quantitative and qualitative) that explored family group decision making (FGDM). In this case, following guidelines for conducting information retrieval as part of Cochrane and Campbell Collaboration systematic reviews, we searched multiple databases for studies relevant to child welfare, child protection, and social care, including: Cochrane Central Register of Controlled Trials (CENTRAL), MEDLINE, PsychInfo; EMBASE, Database of Reviews of Effectiveness (DARE online), Applied Social Sciences (ASSIA), ERIC, CINAHL, International Bibliography of the Social Sciences, Caredata (social work), Social Work Abstracts, Social Sciences Abstracts, Child Abuse and Neglect Database Instrument System (CANDIS), Australian Family and Society Abstracts Database, and Dissertation Abstracts International (DAI). We used a combination of controlled vocabulary and free-test strategies for identifying studies relevant to FGDM, and, because we were interested in both quantitative and qualitative studies, we did not limit our search by including methodological search terms (e.g., qualitative, ethnog). An example of the search terms used in MEDLINE is presented in box 6.4.

In addition to electronic searching, other sources were used to retrieve an exhaustive list of all potential studies, including reference checking, personal communications, hand searching of journals, and gray literature searches. For *reference checking*, we looked at reference lists of all relevant articles that were obtained, including those from previously published reviews on FGDM. Potentially relevant articles were identified and retrieved for potential inclusion in the review. *Personal communication* was conducted by both e-mail and telephone correspondence with authors, presenters, and experts to find any relevant studies not located by other methods. *Hand searching* included searches of journals specific to child maltreatment. Journals hand-searched included: *Child Welfare, Children and Youth Services Review, Social Service Review, Child Maltreatment, Child Abuse and Neglect, Journal of Social Services Research, Social Work, Research*

Box 6.4   Search Terms Used for FGDM Systematic Review in MEDLINE

1. family group.tw.
2. family decision.tw.
3. family decisionmaking.tw.
4. family conferenc$.tw.
5. family unity.tw.
6. family team.tw.
7. group conferenc$.tw.
8. group decision.tw.
9. group decisionmaking.tw.
10. team conferenc$.tw.
11. team decision.tw.
12. team decisionmaking.tw.
13. or/1–12
14. exp child/
15. adolescent/
16. exp infant/
17. (child$or adolescen$or boy$or girl$or infant$or toddler$or baby or babies or preschool$
18. or pre-school or teen$).tw.
19. or/14–17
20. 13 and 18

on Social Work Practice, Social Work Research, and *Child Abuse Review.*
Gray literature sources of potentially relevant studies were also conducted
using gray literature searching techniques and also included search engines
(e.g., Google), selected Web sites relevant to child welfare (e.g., Canadian
Child Welfare Research Portal), clearinghouses for research relevant to
child welfare (e.g., Child Welfare Information Gateway), as well as government Web sites (e.g., The Children's Bureau).

Based on our comprehensive search, we located 1,367 potential hits
relevant to FGDM. Of these, 94 studies were included based on passing
the first-level screening questions, which included: Did the article include
a child protection population? Did the article include a version of family
group conferencing? Is this a study (quantitative/qualitative or both)?
After initial and secondary screening by at least two readers per article,
the final sample contained six quantitative studies (two randomized
and four nonrandomized) that met the inclusion criteria. Fifteen qualitative studies were included in the data extraction phase, each of which
described participants' experiences based on their involvement and perception of FGDM (see Table 6.2).

Table 6.2 Included FGDM Qualitative Studies

Study	Qualitative Approach
Barrera (2006)	Qualitative analytic strategy/content analysis
Bell (2009)	Qualitative summary of interviews
Bell & Wilson (2006)	Theme-based qualitative analysis
Brodie (2008)	Grounded theory
Brown (2007)	Case study analysis
Connolly (2004)	Grounded theory
Connolly (2006)	Grounded theory
Crea & Berzin (2008)	Qualitative summary of interviews
Dawson & Yancey (2006)	Theme-based qualitative analysis
Gallagher & Jasper (2003)	Husserlian phenomenological approach
Holland & O'Neil (2006)	Grounded theory
Holland & Rivett (2008)	Grounded theory
Laws & Kirby (2007)	Theme-based qualitative analysis
McCready & Donnelly (2005)	Theme-based qualitative analysis
Neff (2006)	Grounded theory

KEY POINTS TO REMEMBER

- There is a long-standing debate among qualitative scholars with respect to the utility and influence of literature reviews within qualitative research.
- Similar to the debates involving literature reviews of primary studies, there is no consensus with respect to whether primary qualitative studies should be synthesized and, if so, how this should be done. Some argue for purposive sampling of qualitative studies, and others suggest that systematic reviews of literature provide a comprehensive and transparent process for the identification of all potentially relevant studies.
- Challenges arise when attempting to search for qualitative studies due to limited reporting standards, insufficient indexing for qualitative studies, and untested procedures for using multiple strategies for searching for qualitative studies.
- Because there continue to be many flaws in searching for qualitative methods, it is recommended that, where possible, reviewers avoid indexing and filtering for qualitative designs.
- As demonstrated in our FGDM example, searching within systematic reviews may best be addressed by searching for the substantive research question rather than by study design. With the use of screening levels, qualitative studies can then be separated from other designs for qualitative synthesis.
- Screening should follow systematic review guidelines established by the Cochrane and Campbell Collaborations (e.g., two raters) and should proceed through three stages: (a) initial screening of titles and abstracts, (b) more stringent screening of retrieved texts, (c) data extraction.

SUGGESTED READING

General Readings of Information Retrieval for Qualitative Research

Barroso, J., Gallup, C. J., Sandelowski, M., Meynell, J., Pearce, P. F., & Collins L. J. (2003). The challenge of searching for and retrieving qualitative studies. *Western Journal of Nursing Research, 25*, 153–178.

Booth, A. (1996). In search of the evidence: Informing effective practice. *Journal of Clinical Effectiveness, 1*(1), 25–29.

Dixon-Woods, M, & Fitzpatrick, R. (2001). Qualitative research in systematic reviews. *BMJ, 323,* 765–766.

Dixon-Woods, M, Fitzpatrick, R., & Roberts, K. (2001). Including qualitative research in systematic reviews: Opportunities and problems. *Journal of Evaluation in Clinical Practice, 7*(2), 125–133.

Evans, D. (2002). Database searches for qualitative research. *Journal of the Medical Library Association, 90,* 290–293.

Flemming, K., & Briggs, M. (2007). Electronic searching to locate qualitative research: Evaluation of three strategies. *Journal of Advanced Nursing, 57*(1), 95–100.

Grant, M. J. (2004). How does your searching grow? A survey of search preferences and the use of optimal search strategies in the identification of qualitative research. *Health Information and Libraries Journal, 21*(1), 21–32.

Hartley, J., & Benjamin, M. (1998). An evaluation of structured abstracts in journals published by the British Psychological Society. *British Journal of Educational Psychology, 68,* 443–456.

Holloway, I., & Wheeler, S. (1995). Ethical issues in qualitative nursing research. *Nursing Ethics, 2*(3), 223–232.

Littell, J. H., Corcoran, J., & Pillai, V. (2008). *Systematic reviews and meta-analysis.* New York: Oxford University Press.

Murphy, E., Dingwall, R., Greenbatch, D., Parker, S., & Watson, P. (1998). Qualitative research methods in health technology assessment: A review of the literature. *Health Technology Assessment, 2,* iii-ix, 1–274.

Shaw, R. L., Booth, A., Sutton, A. J., Miller, T., Smith, J. A., Young, B., . . . Dixon-Woods, M. (2004). Finding qualitative research: An evaluation of search strategies. *BMC Medical Research Methodology, 4,* 5.

Indexing Qualitative Research in CINAHL

Wilczynski, N. L., Marks, S., & Haynes, R. B. (2007). Search strategies for identifying qualitative studies in CINAHL. *Qualitative Health Research, 17*(5), 705–710.

Indexing Qualitative Research in MEDLINE

Walters, L. A, Wilczynski, N. L, & Haynes, R. B; (2006). Hedges team. Developing optimal search strategies for retrieving clinically relevant qualitative studies in EMBASE. *Qualitative Health Research, 16*(1), 162–168.

Wong, S. S. L., Wilczynski, N. L., & Haynes, R. B. (2004). Developing optimal search strategies for detecting clinically relevant qualitative studies in Medline. *Medinfo, 107* (Pt 1), 311–316.

Indexing Qualitative Research in PsycInfo

McKibbon, K. A., Wilczynski, N. L., & Haynes, R. B. (2006). Developing optimal search strategies for retrieving qualitative studies in PsycINFO. *Evaluation & the Health* Professions, *29*(4), 440–454.

7

Appraising the Evidence of Qualitative Studies

We have the unappealing double bind whereby qualitative studies can't be verified because researchers don't report on their methodology, and they don't report on their methodology because there are no established cannons or conventions for doing so.

—(Miles & Huberman, 1994, p. 244)

Debates about the inclusion of qualitative research within systematic reviews are nowhere more pronounced than when considering whether common criteria should be developed to assess rigor and credibility of primary studies and what standards should be used to assess the quality of studies. In this chapter, we first offer a sketch of the continuum of views regarding criteria for assessment of quality and rigor paying attention to Padgett's warning (1998) that the use of labels "often obscures the blurriness of categories and can easily verge into name calling" (p. 89). This brief discussion is then followed by our presentation of an assessment tool that we argue allows a researcher to disentangle herself from the thornier and more contentious parts of the debate.

On one end of the continuum, post-positivist positions adopt conventionally established "scientific" criteria of reliability and validity and hold that these standards should be the same for both quantitative and qualitative research. The post-positivist positions promote separate but parallel sets of criteria for qualitative research and quantitative studies, arguing that criteria for assessing qualitative research should relate to the potential for generalizability of findings and the minimization of bias (Hammerley, 1992, qtd in Padgett, 1998).

Given that an interpretivist position begins from the premise that knowledge is both created and contextual as opposed to discovered (Padgett, 1998), for some adherents, this epistemological frame precludes the possibility of developing standardized criteria that can be made applicable across different research contexts. Others within a interpretivist camp have acknowledged the utility of establishing a set of criteria that are unique to qualitative inquiry, and some interpretivist researchers have made attempts to establish general guidelines for assessing quality and rigor in the qualitative research process using such notions as trustworthiness, transferability, and authenticity (see Table 7.1 as an example of one such construction) (Erlandson, Harris, Skipper, & Allen, 1993; Lincoln, 1995; Lincoln & Guba, 1985). However, even within this group of researchers, there remains no consensus on an actual tool to guide decision making in the process of establishing quality. Indeed, there are now over 100 quality appraisal forms to evaluate qualitative research. Many do not distinguish between different epistemological and ontological differences, theoretical frameworks, study designs, and standards for rigor, credibility, and relevance, nor have they themselves been systematically evaluated or explored for relevance to qualitative research

Our position, as we have been proposing throughout, is pragmatic in its orientation and leads us to argue, along with Drisko (1997), for the development of clear evaluative criteria that are responsive to the unique nature of qualitative inquiry.

RELEVANCE OF AN APPRAISAL TOOL ACROSS METHODS

A question remains in the literature whether a single standard of quality can be used for different types of methods or whether different rating criteria are more appropriate for different types of methods, such as ethnography, grounded theory, or phenomenology. Although the development of appraisal tools should involve multiple variations of qualitative methods, we propose that qualitative appraisal tools are important for shedding light on the merits and limitations of qualitative studies on

Table 7.1 Establishing Quality in Qualitative Research

Criterion	Techniques Used to Establish Quality
Truth value/ credibility	Prolonged engagement
	Persistent observation
	Triangulation
	Peer debriefing
	Negative case analysis
	Referential adequacy
	Member checks
	Confirmability
Applicability/ transferability	Sample size addressed
	Thick description
	Reflexive journal
Consistency/ dependability	Audit train
	Congruency in research process
	Consistency of themes and quotes
Neutrality/ confirmability	Use of quotes and examples to support themes
	Consistency of themes and quotes
	Transparency of research process
Face validity/ congruency	Consistent and logical flow of emerging knowledge and experiences
Reflexivity	Researcher's self-awareness
	Attention to personal bias
	Reflexive journaling
Fairness	Reciprocity with participants
	Partnerships with participants in generating knowledge
	Equal access to research process and results
Authenticity	Identification of participants stories, narratives, voices
	Experiences emerge from the participants
	Participant is a "true" participant in research process

Adapted from Quality in qualitative research by L. Lach, T. McNeil, and D. Nicholas, 2005. Unpublished manuscript.

their own terms (Drisko, 1997), and that they can be employed to more reliably gauge the quality of a given study.

THE USE OF APPRAISAL TOOLS TO ASSESS QUALITY

As Sandelowski and Barroso (2007) point out, qualitative synthesis is plagued by the lack of even modest degrees of concordance in reporting styles across peer-reviewed journals, and there is limited journal space in which to adequately address qualitative standards of reporting. Excluding studies based on a rating of quality or on a type of method used in the primary study would present a danger of including inappropriate studies and excluding appropriate ones (Lemmer, Grellier, & Stevens, 1999), given that many articles provide inadequate information about the choice and application of qualitative methods. Not surprisingly, these very same issues come up in quantitative synthesis, and similar methods for coping with inadequate information seem appropriate here. These include contacting authors of highly relevant papers and asking them to fill in the missing pieces that may have been lost during the editing process and attempting to find the larger, more detailed reports on which many published articles are based. Apart from a consideration of these methods for addressing missing information, we present a model that does not exclude studies based on quality, but one in which interpretation of quality itself becomes part of the overall analysis.

QUALITATIVE RESEARCH QUALITY CHECKLIST (QRQC): A MODEL FOR ASSESSING RIGOR AND QUALITY IN QUALITATIVE RESEARCH

The Qualitative Research Quality Checklist (QRQC: Saini, 2011) is a 25-point quality appraisal form designed to evaluate credibility, dependability, confirmability, transferability, authenticity, and relevance of qualitative studies. The QRQC form was created based on existing research regarding the standards for measuring qualitative designs as well as on consultation with experts in the field of qualitative research. The tool was pilot tested at the Factor-Inwentash Faculty of Social Work at the University of Toronto in 2007, and findings were then presented at the Seventh Annual Campbell Collaboration Colloquium in London, England. The pilot study included an analysis of interrater agreement of responses using four masters-level social work classes that completed a QRQC after reading a qualitative study. Modifications were made based on the interrater agreement and on further considerations from the literature regarding indicators of quality in qualitative methods. In fact, like good qualitative research, the development of the QRQC has been an evolving process (see suggested readings at the end of this chapter for a number of articles written about quality and rigor in qualitative research).

The QRQC appraises qualitative studies in terms of their epistemological and theoretical frameworks, study setting, study design, sampling procedures, data collection, ethical issues, reflexivity of the researcher, data analysis, and reporting of the findings. In addition, fairness and promotion of justice are included to evaluate studies for which the central purpose is to empower participants through participant action research. *Not all quality appraisal indicators will be relevant to a study due to differences in the epistemological and ontological stances taken by the authors.* For this reason, QRQC includes three columns for each quality appraisal item. The first column questions whether the quality domain is relevant to the particular study. The second column questions whether there is sufficient information in the study to suggest that it has been addressed in the specific domain of quality. The third column is an open comment box so the reviewer can make interpretive comments about the study and/or of the qualitative domain being assessed and its relevance.

The purpose of these text boxes is to provide the reviewer with the opportunity to write commentaries and explanations of appraisal for each dimension and, at the end, to integrate these into an overall impression of quality. These narrative reflections are important when comparing the quality of multiple qualitative studies, and they can easily be incorporated into the text of the review.

UNDERLYING ASSUMPTIONS OF QRQC

The underlying assumption of this critical appraisal tool is that, regardless of the epistemological or ontological assumptions guiding a particular qualitative study, the "story" should be told in a consistent, transparent way and should adhere to the highest standard of methods associated with the philosophical traditions the investigators purportedly draw from. The story matters, not the discrete ratings of quality. The appraisal tool is not a means of excluding studies based on "quality," but it provides the opportunity to evaluate the quality of studies based on dimensions that have been agreed on by the scientific community.

Discretion, reflection and flexibility remain central, and this provides "guideposts" for evaluating the quality of studies. As such, the interpretation of "quality" becomes part of the reviewer's interpretation of the studies. It is important to move away from the blind utilization of quality tools to justify credibility. At the same time, there is a need for further guidance on ways to assess quality and integrate these interpretations into the analysis. We propose that an interpretative tool with selected guideposts for quality may provide reviewers with the needed flexibility within common standards of quality. The purpose of rating quality in each of these dimensions is not to come up with a total score, nor is the purpose to weigh certain dimensions over others. The QRQC is a method to guide interpretive curiosity about the quality and rigor of included studies, which then contributes to the overall interpretation and synthesis both within and across included studies.

ASSESSING FOR QUALITY USING THE QRQC

The methods for appraisal of qualitative research are based upon an appreciation of different approaches unique to qualitative inquiry coupled with an evaluation (Sandelowski & Barossa, 2007) of quality within qualitative studies. Assessing quality dimensions is based on whether the quality dimension was addressed in the qualitative study and whether the quality dimension was applicable and relevant to the overall focus, approach, and/or design of the study. Including columns for recording whether information was both addressed and applicable provides the opportunity to use the QRQC for a variety of qualitative research methods. For example, if prolonged engagement is not relevant to a grounded theory study, then this dimension would not be applicable to an assessment of quality. Given the complexity of this type of critical assessment of qualitative studies, it is vital that research teams conducting qualitative synthesis include qualitative experts so that this information can be discerned from the primary studies.

QUESTIONS CONSIDERED IN THE QRQC

By proposing an overview of critical appraisal for qualitative research methods, we outline the variations in how quality and credibility are assessed across various qualitative methods. Each question in the QRQC provides a framework for assessing the overall quality of the included studies. Not all questions will be answered by the content in the published reports, given the limits imposed on authors by journal guidelines for publication. Therefore, reviewers are encouraged to contact the authors of the included studies to gather additional information not found in the published reports (see Box 7.1 for a proposed template for requesting information from authors).

We present our assessment of quality of two qualitative studies (Bell & Wilson, 2006; Holland & O'Neil, 2006) included in our FGDM review. The first, by Bell and Wilson (2006), reported on a qualitative study using a theme-based qualitative analysis to explore the experiences of 20 families who participated in a family group conference pilot project in the United Kingdom. The second study, by Holland and O'Neill (2006), recorded the findings from a qualitative research initiative exploring family group conferencing in Wales. We e-mailed the primary authors of both studies to ask specific questions about: (a) the qualitative method guiding the study, (b) the philosophical framework guiding the inquiry, (c) the characteristics of the sample, (d) additional information about the data collection methods, (e) the process for data analysis, (f) the authors' subjective experience, and (g) whether there were any other contextual factors that were important but were not expressed in the report.

Is the Purpose and Research Question Stated Clearly?

The first question relates to the overall purpose of the research question and allows the researcher to determine whether the topic is important,

---

Box 7.1   Template for Requesting Information from Authors of Included Studies

Dear author,
Along with my colleagues, I am participating in a qualitative synthesis on (name of project). The purpose of the qualitative synthesis is to explore (include purpose of the project). We have included your qualitative study (name of study) in our sample of included studies. We have a some questions about your study that we hope you could answer for us so we can better understand the context of the study and the factors that are not clear to us (we find that journals often put limits on the length of qualitative papers, which leaves the authors deciding what to include and what to leave out). We hope you can take the time to reply to these questions so we can integrate your comments into our analysis.

relevant, and of interest for a given question. It is common for authors to briefly state the research question in the abstract of the article and again in more detail in the introduction. It may be phrased as a research question or it may be described as the general purpose for conducting the study. The purpose of qualitative research is often concerned with an exploration and/or observation of a phenomenon, a discovery of needs, and/or an in-depth understanding of experiences and perceptions.

We indicated that the article from Bell and Wilson (2006) did pose a clear research question, which we found to be applicable to the study. The study focuses specifically on the views of the children who attended the FDGM conferences and discusses the issue of how to involve them and address their needs within the conference process. The issue to be addressed in this study is how or whether children can be involved in the process of decision making and planning to achieve change in a way that is empowering to them. A more specific aim was to assess the experiences of the children and to evaluate whether their attendance at the conference was helpful and led to improvements in family relationships and in their relationships with professionals. Holland and O'Neill (2006) also posed a clear statement for their qualitative study. In this study, the authors sought to consider the children's perspectives of being involved in FGDM and to learn about their experiences.

Is a Qualitative Approach Appropriate to Answer the Research Question?

This question relates to whether using qualitative methods is the most appropriate research to answer the research question. Qualitative methods are influenced by various theoretical perspectives, but most qualitative research methods are used to interpret, illuminate, illustrate, and explore meaning, context, unanticipated phenomena, process, opinions, attitudes, actions, and to assist the researcher to learn about people who are few or hard to reach. Qualitative research is also best for answering questions that: explore a topic about which little is known, pursue topics of sensitivity and emotional depth, capture the "lived experience" of those in a particular situation, are geared toward getting inside the "black box" of programs and interventions, move the field beyond a quantitative impasse in explaining findings, and seek to merge activism with research (Padgett, 1998). Drisko (1998) states that identifying the philosophical framework underpinning the study is considered an important criterion for assessing the internal consistency of the study. Once a philosophical framework is selected, the research should then be consistently linked to the chosen framework. In these studies, however, no framework was put forward and no guiding method was chosen. However, discourse analysis can be used as a method to reveal this latent content of the philosophical stance and its consistency of application. Another strategy may be to contact the primary authors to request this information.

Holland and O'Neill (2006) provide a clear case for the need to include children's views within the current knowledge base of FGDM. They report that most research in this area has focused on quantitative outcomes of whether the intervention works. Consequently, there has been little attention made to the inclusion of children's voices and their perspectives of being involved in these interventions. Based on a critical realist approach, the authors interviewed several attendees from each conference in an attempt to gain access to a balanced picture of what "really" happened at the conference. Nonetheless, there was an overt acknowledgment that the style of interviewing would explore participants' social constructions of the event and its place in their lives, rather than a simple factual recall. In assessing the article from Bell and Wilson (2006), it seems that using qualitative research was consistent with the research questions of the study, given that the purpose was to explore the views of the children involved in FGDM. The authors point out that more research is needed to explore the actual benefits and costs to children of active involvement, and to identify how safe and effective engagement can be achieved.

Is the Setting of the Study Appropriate and Specific for Exploring the Research Question?

The contextual focus of qualitative research suggests that a qualitative study should provide enough information about the setting of the study to provide a rich description of where the study was conducted, who was involved in the study, the length of time in the setting, and the contextual factors of the setting to allow consumers to consider the transferability of findings to other similar settings (Drisko, 1998; Greene, 1994). Moreover, the relevancy of the setting or context to the task of assessing transferability is further explored by taking into consideration the objectives, purposes, expected audiences, and the philosophical framework guiding the study.

Holland and O'Neill (2006) and Bell and Wilson (2006) both make compelling arguments that research is needed to consider the views of the children involved in FGDM within the background of increased emphasis on children's participation and views. For both studies, more attention to the philosophical frameworks guiding these studies would have assisted in distilling the range of viewpoints of children's experiences.

Is There Prolonged Engagement to Render the Inquirer Open to Multiple Influences?

Prolonged engagement refers to both (a) the history of involvement with the groups under study, with the presumption that increased involvement allows for trust building and a consequent comfort of participants in sharing more nuanced and "truthful" stories, and (b) a lengthy process of data collection that can enhance breadth and nuance of perspective (Padgett, 2008).

Holland and O'Neill's (2006) interviews were between 50 and 90 minutes, although not all of the time would have been taken up with the formal interview part. Holland (e-mail correspondence, June 8, 2011) notes that the interviewer had the challenge of interviewing children she had not met before, so she needed to build trust and dialogue very quickly prior to the interview. She played some simple games with the younger ones to begin this process. Of the interviews that took place with the parents in the home, the majority of the adults left the room when the interview took place. Those who stayed for part of the interviews encouraged the children to speak and have their say. The authors note that this seemed to help the younger children as it seemed to give them permission to engage. Some of the interviews had other children in the room or another adult (e.g., aunt). However, there is the possibility that children did not feel at ease with sharing their experiences of being involved in the FGDM process, given that they were interviewed only once with adults present.

Is There Persistent Observation in the Setting to Focus on the Issues Relevant to the Research Question?

Persistent observation refers to there being enough information to allow the reader to assess whether there is sufficient depth of data collection to permit an appreciation of the complexity of a phenomenon. Lincoln and Guba (1985) describe persistent observation stating that:

> If the purpose of prolonged engagement is to render the inquirer open to the multiple influences—the mutual shapers and contextual factors— that impinge upon the phenomenon being studied, the purpose of persistent observation is to identify those characteristics and elements in the situation that are most relevant to the problem or issue being pursued and focusing on them in detail. If prolonged engagement provides scope, persistent observation provides depth (p. 304).

Bell and Wilson (2006) interviewed children 6 weeks after involvement in the intervention. The duration of time on the children's experiences have unknown influences, especially given that younger children (as young as 6 years old) may have had difficulty recalling their previous experiences and their perception of these experiences may have changed as time passed. Holland and O'Neill (2006) interviewed all children once, 1 month after the intervention and then interviewed 13 of the children a second time, 6 months later. Holland (e-mail correspondence, June 8, 2011) notes that sometimes it worked better if interviews took place soon after the conference, as this helped minimize the difficulties some children had recalling the process when interviews were conducted sometime after the conference. However, some children were negative immediately after the conference as the event was still raw. In this case, leaving a gap between the conference and interview may have helped because many of the actions that young people were pessimistic about happening did happen, as was reflected in the review meetings.

Is There Compatibility Between Research Question, Method Chosen, and Research Design?

The research question should guide the qualitative approach, the methods used in the study, and the overall research design, including the nature of the sample, data collection, and methods of analysis (Drisko, 1998; Padgett, 2008). Coffey and Atkinson (1996) report, "there is a variety in techniques because there are different questions to be addressed and different versions of social reality" (p. 14). Indeed, as we have been emphasizing throughout, qualitative research is not a single unified tradition, but instead it is a family of related approaches with different purposes, epistemologies, and methods (Drisko, 1998).

Holland and O'Neill (2006) state that they used "mainly qualitative research methods" (p. 97). Bell and Wilson (2006) do not follow a formal method of inquiry for the study. Not including a method to guide the inquiry makes it difficult to assess the study's consistency with any single philosophical framework (Drisko, 1998).

Is the Process of the Sample Selection Adequately Described and Consistent With the Research Design/Research Question?

Sampling in qualitative research is often purposeful and the process used to select participants should be clearly described. Purposive sampling selects participants for a specific reason (e.g., age, culture, experiences), based on the purpose of the study and the methods chosen to guide the data collection and analysis. There is a range of sampling techniques used in qualitative research, depending on the purpose of method the qualitative study (Miles & Huberman, 1994; Onwuegbuzie & Leech, 2007b). In *quota sampling,* the researcher selects specific characteristics for the study and then samples potential participants, based on these, for inclusion in the study. *Quota* refers to having a set number of participants with specific characteristics (e.g., 5 mothers and 5 fathers receiving parenting education). *Snowball sampling,* also known as network sampling, involves asking participants already selected for the study to refer other potential participants. *Maximum variation sampling* selects a wide range of individuals, groups, or settings. *Homogenous sampling* uses a small sample with similar characteristics. *Critical case sampling* employs key participants to bring out the experiences of a critical case. *Theory-based sampling* includes participants based on theory development. *Extreme case sampling* includes participants with more extreme characteristics. *Typical case sampling,* in contrast to extreme case sampling, samples participants with typical experiences in order to gain consensus. The sampling strategy used should depend on the purpose and method of the qualitative study. For example, phenomenological methods to explore participants' experiences of a single event may require only a few selected individuals who have experienced the event. Grounded theory methods to explore a theoretical understanding most often include a range of experiences and views about the event (Drisko, 1998). Regardless of the chosen sample strategy, the study should explicitly state the method used and the rationale of the sampling strategy should fit with the study question and the method guiding the study.

In the study by Holland and O'Neill (2006), 17 family group conferences (FGCs) were evaluated in depth. The sample frame was a prospective, universal sample of all FGDMs that took place in a 12-month period of one FGDM project. This project provided all FGDM services to three local authority geographical areas. There were 18 FGDMs during the time period, and in all but 1 of these, the families consented to take part in the research. Inclusion criteria were: (a) consent from the child, young person, and main caregiver to be interviewed, and (b) interventions that went to a full conference (Holland, e-mail correspondence, June 8, 2011). In the study by Bell and Wilson (2006), the first 20 families offered FGDM were included in the sample. It remains unclear what influence the sample selection may have had on the findings. Because there is no qualitative method to guide the study, it is unclear whether the strategy of choosing the first 20 families fit with the research question or method.

Is the Sample Size and Composition Justified and Appropriate for the Method/Research Design/Research Question?

Most qualitative studies use small-scale sample sizes but the actual number of participants will range based on the chosen method of the study. Qualitative sampling is often flexible, and it usually evolves as the study progresses until the point of redundancy in emerging themes has been reached. In general, qualitative samples should not be too small so to achieve redundant themes, but they should not be too large so to make rich case analysis difficult (Onwuegbuzie & Leech, 2007c; Sandelowski, 1995). Creswell (1998, 2002) recommends guidelines for qualitative sample sizes: ethnography might include 1 cultural sharing group; case studies might include 3 to 5 cases; grounded theory may include 20 to 30 people; and phenomenological studies may include 10 participants in in-depth interviews. *Composition justification* refers to the appropriateness of the sample "study parameters, including settings, context, locations, times, events, incidents activities, experiences and/or social processes" (Onwuegbuzie & Leech, 2007a, p. 117). The composition of the study considers who was, and who was not, included in the sample and a consideration for why (e.g., age, gender, ethnicity, relationship status) some participants were included and others not included.

In the study by Holland and O'Neill (2006), they began by interviewing 25 children 1 month after the FGC and then 13 of these children 6 months later. Children's ages ranged between 6 and 18 years and none of these children were involved in formal child-protection cases. The investigators note that several of the children had learning disabilities, and one child was profoundly deaf. In the study by Bell and Wilson (2006), 20 families were selected for the interviews. Of the included children, two were aged 6 years; seven were aged between 10 and 16 years. No information was provided regarding culture, race, socioeconomic status, the nature of the families' involvement with child-protection services, the children's residency, location, whether the children were attending school, and so on. Overall, this lack of detail about the sample composition makes it difficult to get a sense of the samples included in these studies, which has implications for later synthesis.

Are the Methods for Data Collection Consistent With the Research Question?

In qualitative research, data are collected through a variety of strategies, including interviews, focus groups, participant observations, reviews of published reports, historical records, textual analysis, memos, and artifacts. A central issue in the credibility of qualitative studies is the description of how and under what conditions the research data was collected (Drisko, 1998). Reporting offered by the researcher should include sufficient information regarding the data collection methods and should describe how these methods were used in the data collection phase.

Holland and O'Neill (2006) completed in-depth interviews with the children, usually at the children's home. In Bell and Wilson's (2006) study, they conducted interviews 6 weeks after the children attended FGDM. They report that other data collection efforts included referral information for the families and whether they had previous contact with social services. Another data collection method included receiving copies of all FGDM completed plans.

Are the Methods for Data Collection Consistent With the Method/Research Design/Research Question?

There are no steadfast rules about methods for data collection; however, some guiding assumptions can be made within the various research designs that are associated with different methods, and this leads toward congruency. For *phenomenological* studies, data collection methods usually include in-depth interviews, each lasting approximately 2 hours and followed by self-reflections of the researcher. In *ethnographic* studies, the researcher usually collects descriptions of behaviors through observations, interviews, documents, and artifacts. In *case study* analyses, the researcher builds an in-depth picture of the case by using documents, archival records, interviews, and observations. In *grounded theory* methods for collection, the researcher develops a model or theory with saturating categories and often uses interviews, reflective journals, focus groups, and observations.

In Bell and Wilson's (2006) study, the children were given a "child-friendly, brief questionnaire comprising straightforward questions about how comfortable and happy or sad they felt about their experience of the conference, their degree of understanding of what was happening, their sense of involvement in the process and whether they felt they could say everything they wanted" (p. 675). Six weeks after a conference, interviews were held to gain richer and more detailed accounts of the children's experience and views after some time had passed. Although both questionnaires and interviews were used, it is unclear how these were integrated or interpreted and whether they were combined or considered separately. Holland and O'Neill (2006) completed a range of interview methods designed to engage the children. These included a facial expressions exercise to relay their emotions and feelings on different aspects and stages of their FGDM, and to gain insight into participation levels and roles within the FGDM. Drawing materials, stickers, figurines, and other techniques were also used. In addition, children were asked to develop their ideal forum for decision making and to give advice to a friend about FGDMs. All children agreed to complete a questionnaire at both interviews and to conduct a card-sorting exercise expressing their priorities for a family meeting.

Is a Range of Methods Used for Triangulation?

Triangulation occurs when researchers seek corroboration between two or more sources for data interpretation. Padgett (2008) describes triangulation as a reliance on multiple sources of information to achieve a comprehensive picture of a fixed point of reference. Although Padgett (2008) points out that triangulation has been rejected by some interpretivist researchers on the grounds that there is no singular reference point to consider, she notes that triangulation remains a common method used in social work to enhance rigor in qualitative research. Triangulation methods include: data analyzed by colleagues who hold contrasting theoretical orientations; use of more than one qualitative method (or mix-method); use of multiple observers/multiple coders; use of more than one data source (e.g., interviews and observations); and use of interdisciplinary triangulation by using a team of researchers from different fields (Denzin, 1978; Padgett, 2008).

Bell and Wilson (2006) used two methods for data collection, interviews and questionnaires, and it appears that some integration of these was completed in the analysis. For example, they state that "those who felt positive had, as described in their questionnaires, found the atmosphere comfortable, had enjoyed the food and had clearly benefited from seeing the family trying to solve some of their problems together" (p. 676). Methods for triangulation provide suggestions of consistency across methods chosen, and these seem compatible with the aims of the studies. In Holland and O'Neill's (2006) study, Holland (e-mail correspondence, June 8, 2011) noted that there was an element of triangulation in that the semistructured interviews included the gathering of baseline data, including a scale to assess strengths and difficulties and school attendance. Young people's views of how their lives had been affected in the follow-up interviews were compared with their responses to these measures at follow-up. They also used a diamond ranking exercise regarding priorities in a FGDM that provided a reasonably effective way of displaying differences and similarities of views across different participant groups.

Is There an Articulation of Who Collected the Data, When the Data Was Collected, and Who Analyzed the Data?

In qualitative research, transparency of data collection method is important, given the subjective location of experiences in qualitative research and the connections with the researcher to the process and interpretations of the results. Transparency of data collection methods includes providing information about who was involved in each phase of the study. For example, if researchers hire research assistants—individuals who may or may not have adequate prior knowledge of the phenomena—to complete interviews, the authors of the study should clearly indicate how this may have influenced the data collection and subsequent analysis. By remaining transparent, the reader can better assess the level of reflective analysis at each of these stages.

All interviews in the studies conducted by Holland and O'Neill (2006) and Bell and Wilson (2006) were completed by one of the authors. This information is particularly important for this study given the required skills needed to interview young children about their experiences. Special considerations for interviewing children include: the timing of the interviews, the types of questions being asked, the level of comprehension required to understand and respond to the questions, the ability of the researcher to ask questions at a comfortable pace for the children involved, and the ability of the researcher to engage children without influencing their experiences with misleading questions (Parkinson & Cashmore, 2007).

Is There an Audit Trail Regarding Data Collection Including Tapes, Memos, and Note Taking of Decisions Made in The Study?

Leaving an audit trail refers to the researcher leaving a paper trail of field notes, transcripts of interviews, reflective journals, administrative journals, and memos documenting decisions. The purpose of the audit trail is to provide a transparent data collection process for others to scrutinize the steps taken in the research and for others to confirm findings based on the documents provided (Lincoln & Guba, 1985). Audit trails help to assess whether reactivity and biases of the researcher were adequately addressed during the study and what influences these may have had on the overall findings. Padgett (2004) states that leaving an audit trail is done in the spirit of openness. Audit trails also allow others to consider the rigor of the study. Inui and Frankel (1991) suggest that auditing the work of others allows for verification that the findings are grounded in the data, that the coded themes are logical and credible, and that steps in the research process are fully explained and a strong rationale is provided.

Holland and O'Neill (2006) used qualitative data analysis software (Atlas.ti) for all qualitative data management and analysis. Bell and Wilson (2006) used a few verbatim comments in the findings section. These authors make no mention of using an audit trail. Not using an audit trail has implications for the overall credibility of the findings. Moreover, in this study, it would have been particularly important to use an audit trail given that there is limited description of the steps taken in the study and because there appears to be no guiding method to frame this inquiry.

Is There Adequate Consideration of Ethical Issues, Such as Informed Consent, Privacy, and Confidentiality and Protection From Harm?

Qualitative studies should conform to research ethics (Drisko, 1998). Researchers should describe steps taken regarding ethical considerations, including how informed consent was obtained. If children or other vulnerable groups make up the sample, special provisions must often be made. A statement that an ethics review board has approved the study is sometimes sufficient. Researchers might also describe procedures for ensuring privacy and confidentiality, including how these were ensured and maintained during and after the study.

Holland and O'Neill (2006) stated that ethical issues were considered especially important in their study given that it included a vulnerable population. Informed consent was achieved at a number of stages during the study. In Bell and Wilson (2006) study, there is no indication of whether ethics was obtained for this study. Privacy in this study is questionable given that other people were coming into the interview location and making comments during the children's interviews.

Has the Researcher Identified Potential and Actual Biases (Both as Researcher and in the Research Design)?

Qualitative researchers need to explicitly identify sources of potential bias, including, for example, whether they have initial expectations of study results, as this strengthens the credibility and applicability of the findings (Drisko, 1998). Researchers should provide enough description of their roles in the research design, their understanding of their roles within the production of knowledge, and how the process of the research might have shaped the results. Qualitative researchers seek to acknowledge biases and explore, through self-awareness, the potential influence that they may bring to the production of qualitative studies (Drisko, 1998).

According to the biographies reported in the two studies, the authors are both teachers and researchers. Holland (e-mail correspondence,

June 8, 2011) noted that the researchers were children's advocates with a separate FGDM project at the time. This appeared to have had a positive influence, as the researchers were familiar with the FGDM process, which helped them probe for follow-on questions.

Did the Researcher(S) Use a Reflexive Journal in the Data Analysis and Interpretation?

One way to document the potential bias of researchers within a study is to use reflexive journaling prior, during, and after data collection. Identification of potential biases recorded in reflexive journaling requires substantial self-reflection and self-analysis to explore possible biases emerging from the journaling process. Therefore, credibility is enhanced when researchers document any potential biases and how these many have influenced or contributed to the limitations of the findings (Drisko, 1998).

There was no mention of reflexivity in the studies conducted by Bell and Wilson (2006) and Holland and O'Neill (2006) and no indication that either study used a reflexive journal. Holland (e-mail correspondence, June 8, 2011) stated that memos were used following each interview to record impressions and feelings about each encounter and these were explored, with the principal investigator, in regular supervision sessions in which issues of bias were discussed.

Is the Process of Data Analysis Presented With Sufficient Detail and Depth to Provide Insight Into the Meanings and Perceptions of the Sample?

In qualitative data analysis, codes serve to label, separate, compile, and organize. Methods for transforming raw data into codes will depend on the method used in the analysis and the purpose of the research. For example, in *phenomenological analysis,* the researcher begins with a full description of the phenomenon. Individual experiences are listed; each statement is treated as having equal worth; and the researcher works to develop a list of nonrepetitive, nonoverlapping statements. These statements are then grouped into "meaning units." The researcher then constructs an overall description of the meaning and the essence of the experience. In *ethnographic analysis,* the analysis often begins with a description of the setting and events, then searches for patterned regularities in the data, followed by interpretation of the culture-sharing group. In *case study analysis,* the researcher often first describes the boundaries and characteristics of the case, then collects instances from the data so that issue-relevant meanings will emerge. This is often followed by direct interpretation where meanings emerge from pulling the data apart and then by establishing patterns and looking for correspondence between two or more categories. In *grounded theory,* the researcher often begins with open coding by developing categories of information and reducing the data to a set of concepts. This is followed by axial coding whereby the researcher creates a coding paradigm that visually portrays the interrelationships of these axial coding categories of information. The researcher then conducts selective coding by building a story that connects the categories and abstracted theoretical constructs based on these relationships. Regardless of the method used for data analysis, there should be sufficient description to allow the reader to assess whether data analysis was based on and was consistent with the method and purpose of the study.

Bell and Wilson (2006) described their data analysis as "theme-based qualitative analysis" (p. 675). This leaves a gap in the connection of their data analysis to a qualitative method and epistemological stance. Holland and O'Neill (2006) stated that initial codes were generated from a previous pilot study, relevant literature, and the team's reading of the initial data. Codes were then added as the data analysis progressed. The investigators used cross-coder reliability by double-checking some of the initial interviews. The analysis was carried out on a cross-case and intracase basis with a search for exceptions.

Are Quotes Used to Match Concepts and Themes Derived From the Raw Data?

Quoted words and phrases from participants are a common feature of qualitative research studies (Sandelowski, 1994). Quotes allow the reader to assess whether these quotes match concepts and themes presented by the researchers. Corden and Sainsbury (2006) identify common reasons for including quotes in qualitative reports: (a) qualitative studies are tied to narrative traditions so including quotes is consistent with this method of inquiry; (b) quotes can be included as evidence of the consistency of the interpretations with the words and phrases expressed by the participants; (c) quotes can also help to further explain and illustrate key messages in the findings; (d) using the verbatim comments from the participants can also lead to a deeper understanding of the themes;(e) quotes give participants a voice in the report; and (f) verbatim comments serve to enhance the readability of the reports.

Bell and Wilson (2006) and Holland and O'Neill (2006) both provide short quotes to illustrate the major themes in the studies. The use of quotes in these studies seems to support other findings that emerged from other sources (e.g., questionnaires).

Do the Findings Emerge From the Experiences of the Sample?

The findings should help the reader understand how the themes emerged from the experiences of the participants or from the influences of the researcher. Lincoln and Guba (1985), for example, state that the "design of a naturalistic inquiry . . . can not be given in advance; it must emerge, develop and unfold" (p. 225). In other words, a researcher's preconceived notions and personal opinions can dramatically influence findings if these biases and assumptions emanating from subjective positioning remain unexplored throughout the research process (Padgett, 2008).

Holland and O'Neill (2006) only report on the findings from the first interviews conducted with the children within 1 month of the FGDM. The data from the 6-month follow-up is reported elsewhere. In the study from Bell and Wilson (2006), there are many unanswered questions about the researchers' involvement in the study, their personal opinions about FGDM, and whether they have any connection to the FGDM program that may influence their thoughts about the program. More information about these important questions are needed, especially given that findings were mostly positive, even though some children did not seem to benefit as much as others. These negative cases were not adequately addressed in the findings and did not adequately emerge from the findings.

Was Member Checking Employed?

Member checking includes asking participants to confirm or disconfirm the accuracy of the researcher's observations and interpretations and to solicit their views about the credibility of the findings and interpretations (Creswell, 1998). Member checking involves presenting the themes and findings derived from the data analysis back to the participants for their assessment of the accuracy of the interpretations and findings. Lincoln and Guba (1985) consider member checking to be "the most critical technique for establishing credibility" (p. 314).

There is no indication that Bell and Wilson (2006) used member checking with the children in their study. Holland and O'Neill (2006) shared emerging conclusions at a project management meeting composed of professionals and family members as a means of providing an informal element of participant validation.

Does the Researcher Provide a "Thick Description" of the Sample and Results in Order to Appraise Transferability?

Thick description allows the reader to make decisions regarding the transferability of findings (Creswell, 1998; Erlandson, Harris, Skipper, & Allen, 1993; Lincoln & Guba, 1985; Merriam, 1988) by providing sufficient details about the context, setting, and participants included in the study. For example, by carefully describing the sample and using examples from the text (e.g., quoting the participants) to support conclusions, the reader is provided with the context needed to assess whether the findings emerged from the data and whether these findings might be applicable to samples in similar settings. In determining whether these findings can be transferred to settings, there must be sufficient detail about the study sample and how such details relate to the findings.

In both the studies by Bell and Wilson (2006) and Holland and O'Neill (2006), the authors do not provide adequate information to assess the potential transferability of findings to other similar settings. There are many missing pieces of these stories, so it is difficult to assess the potential for transferability of themes to other similar contexts. Caution must be made before integrating these findings with other interviews with children, given the concerns raised throughout this appraisal.

ADDITIONAL ITEMS (IF APPLICABLE TO PURPOSE OF THE STUDY) FOR EXPLICITLY JUSTICE-ORIENTED OR PARTICIPATORY ACTION RESEARCH

When one of the study's purposes is to empower people to take effective action toward improving conditions in their lives, such as in participatory action research, additional criteria for evaluating the quality of qualitative studies would be considered, including a focus on authenticity, fairness, and justice. As these were not included as intentions for Bell and Wilson's (2006) study, none of these are applicable in the appraisal of their study.

Were Stakeholders Involved in the Project?

Qualitative studies involving stakeholders should describe the involvement of stakeholders throughout the project. For the study to be participatory, stakeholders should be involved in the decision processes to identify the issue/problem/need examined by the study and the best research question to understand the issue/problem/need of those affected. Stakeholders should also be involved in all parts of the research design, implementation, collection of data, analysis, findings, and dissemination of the results. Community-based participatory research often produces competing explanations that reflect multiple perceptions of reality, and the presentation of findings should reflect these differences.

Did all Stakeholders Have Equal Access to the Research Process and Benefits?

Knowledge produced by social science research is a powerful and effective means to influence decisions about everyday lives (Guyette, 1983; Hall, 1979; Reinharz, 1979; St. Denis, 2004). Whether the influence of research is detrimental or supportive to a group often depends on who controls the research process (St. Denis, 2004: 292). Within this framework, communities without sociopolitical power can use research to support their struggles for self-determination and gain control of information that can influence decisions about their lives. Community-based participatory research is rooted in justice-oriented human interactions. If the community is actively involved in developing recommendations, the process is more likely to have an impact on the community.

Did Stakeholders Enhance Their Understanding of Their Own Reality as Part of the Research Process and Results?

Within this framework, knowledge for the sake of knowledge is futile and social science must be committed to social change. The study should address how the research considers the welfare of the people involved and how this is related to community need. In this regard, researchers are challenged to do research for and with people rather than on or about the people.

Are the Stakeholders Empowered to Act as a Result of the Research Process?

Within this framework, the study should demonstrate how people were empowered to take effective action toward improving conditions in their lives (Park, Brydon-Miller, Hall, & Jackson, 1993). Evidence of action within the qualitative study may include: (a) nurturing growth in people, (b) abolishing unjust policies, and (c) constructing new ideas and structures. Participatory action research is not neutral. Participatory action research studies should demonstrate how the research is being used to eliminate injustice and oppression. In this sense, action research is explicitly understood as being politically motivated and driven.

OVERALL IMPRESSIONS OF THE QUALITY OF THE INCLUDED STUDIES

In the implications section of the study by Bell and Wilson (2006), the researchers state that "on the evidence of the children involved in this small study, FGCs [FGDM] can provide a valuable and valued resource" (p. 675). Based on our appraisal of the quality of this study, a more tentative and cautious tone is needed when discussing the implications due to the presence of several critical methodological limitations, as well as the lack of detail regarding the context, setting, and experiences of the children. Similarly, when the researchers state that "based on the experiences of the children in this project, children's inclusion in FGCs [FGDM] is generally to be encouraged" (p. 675), this seems to be a generalization that cannot and should not be made given that this is a qualitative design that does not adequately address the potential for the transferability of knowledge to other similar children. Also of interest are the negative cases that were presented but not explained. In a high quality qualitative analysis, it is important to explore these experiences. For example, the statement that revealed that the child respondent was "feeling just mixed up" (p. 678) after attending the intervention is worthy of commentary and further analysis. Findings, although largely positive, did not explore the full range of experiences shared by the children. There are a number of methodological issues that raise substantial concerns, as explored herein, and it would be important to consider these issues when deciding how to integrate this information with other studies that have similarly explored the experiences of children involved in this intervention.

Holland and O'Neill (2006) provide an in-depth study of a small number of children involved in FGDM. The findings are exploratory but demonstrate insightful themes about children's participation. Although most experiences they cite are positive, other participants felt distressed or disempowered by their participation in FGDM, especially those who witnessed serious arguments in the meetings. This study also sheds light on the difference between children's experiences of being listened to being involved in the decision making.

SUMMARY OF QUALITY APPRAISAL

Within the family of qualitative methods, epistemological frameworks often shape how quality is assessed (Padgett, 1998). There is no universal standard for assessing qualitative criteria and there are ongoing debates about how to assess the rigor and credibility of qualitative studies. We have proposed an overarching approach for assessing quality that requires careful consideration for the uniqueness of various methods, designs, purposes, and epistemological frameworks. Depending also on the purpose of the qualitative synthesis, researchers may place more or less emphasis on different aspects of quality. Although we have tried to detail some of the more common elements, it remains the responsibility of the consumer of research to assess the potential transferability of findings based on a careful analysis of the applicability of findings from one setting to the another.

KEY POINTS TO REMEMBER

- Assessing the quality of qualitative studies remains a contested area of debate among researchers.
- There are now over 100 quality appraisal forms to evaluate qualitative research, but few have been tested in terms of their ability to appraise the quality of qualitative research.

- Including some assessment of quality is important for conducting qualitative synthesis given that some decisions will need to be made on how to include studies of various qualities.
- We propose the use of an overarching appraisal guide that is flexible enough to accommodate various qualitative methods.
- Studies should be appraised according to the required elements of their respective epistemologies and methods. Failure to identify core stances and methods often means that quality is difficult to appraise (and may be considered by some to indicate lower quality).
- Studies of lesser quality should not be excluded in the analysis. Rather, they should be included in order to add to the richness of the findings, keeping in mind the strengths and limitations of each included study.

SUGGESTED READING

Anastas, J. W. (2004). Quality in qualitative evaluation: Issues and possible answers. *Research on Social Work Practice, 14*(1), 57–65.

Anfara, V. A., Jr., Brown, K. M., & Mangione, T. L. (2002). Qualitative analysis on stage: Making the research process more public. *Educational Researcher, 31*(7), 28–38.

Angen, M. J. (2000). Evaluating interpretive inquiry: Reviewing the validity debate and opening the dialogue. *Qualitative Health Research, 10*(3), 378–395.

Bailey, P. H. (1996). Assuring quality in narrative analysis. *Western Journal of Nursing Research, 18*(2), 186–194.

Boulton, M., & Fitzpatrick, R. (1994). Quality in qualitative research. *Critical Public Health, 5*(3), 19–26.

Carnevale, F. A. (2002). Authentic qualitative research and the quest for methodological rigour. *Canadian Journal of Nursing Research, 34*(2), 121–128.

Charmaz, K. (2004). Premises, principles, and practices in qualitative research: Revisiting the foundations. *Qualitative Health Research, 14*(7), 976–993.

Creswell, J. W., & Miller, D. L. (2000). Determining validity in qualitative inquiry. *Theory into Practice, 39*(3), 124–131.

Cutcliffe, J. R., & McKenna, H. P. (1999). Establishing the credibility of qualitative research findings: The plot thickens. *Journal of Advanced Nursing, 30*(2), 374–380.

Dixon-Woods, M., Shaw, R. L., Agarwal, S., & Smith, J. A. (2004). The problem of appraising qualitative research. *Quality & Safety in Health Care, 13*(3), 223–225.

Drisko, J. (1997). Strengthening qualitative studies and reports: Standards to enhance academic integrity. *Journal of Social Work Education, 33*, 1–13.

Finlay, L. (2002). "Outing" the researcher: The provenance, process, and practice of reflexivity. *Qualitative Health Research, 12*(4), 531–545.

Forchuk, C., & Roberts, J. (1993). How to critique qualitative health research articles. *Canadian Journal of Nursing Research, 25*(4), 47–56.

Karim, K. (2001). Assessing the strengths and weaknesses of action research. *Nursing Standard, 15*(26), 33–35.

Koch, T. (1994). Establishing rigour in qualitative research: The decision trail. *Journal of Advanced Nursing, 19*, 976–986.

Lazaraton, A. (2003). Evaluative criteria for qualitative research in applied linguistics: Whose criteria and whose research? *The Modern Language Journal, 87*(1), 1–12.

Madill, A., Jordan, A., & Shirley, C. (2000). Objectivity and reliability in qualitative analysis: Realist, contextualist and radical constructionist epistemologies. *British Journal of Psychology, 91*(1), 1–20.

Mays, N., & Pope, C. (1995). Qualitative research: Rigour and qualitative research. *BMJ, 311*(6997), 109–112.

Morse, J. M., & Singleton, J. (2001). Exploring the technical aspects of "fit" in qualitative research. *Qualitative Health Research, 11*(6), 841–847.

Parker, I. (2004). Criteria for qualitative research in psychology. *Qualitative Research in Psychology, 1*(2), 95–106.

Patton, M. Q. (1999). Enhancing the quality and credibility of qualitative analysis. *Health Services Research, 34*(5), 1189–1209.

Peck, E., & Secker, J. (1999). Quality criteria for qualitative research: Does context make a difference? *Qualitative Health Research, 9*(4), 552–558.

Power, R. (2001). Checklists for improving rigour in qualitative research. Never mind the tail (checklist), check out the dog (research). *BMJ, 323*(7311), 514–515.

Reid, A., & Gough, S. (2000). Guidelines for reporting and evaluating qualitative research: What are the alternatives? *Environmental Education Research, 6*(1), 59–90.

Rubin, A. (2000). Standards for rigor in qualitative inquiry. *Research on Social Work Practice, 10*(2), 173–179.

Shenton, A. K. (2004). Strategies for ensuring trustworthiness in qualitative research projects. *Education for Information, 22*(2), 63–75.

Smith, J. K., & Deemer, D. K. (2000). The problem of criteria in the age of relativism. In N. K. Denzin & Y. S. Lincoln (Eds.), *Handbook of qualitative research* (2nd ed., pp. 877–896). Thousand Oaks, CA: Sage.

Sparkes, A. C. (2001). Myth 94: Qualitative health researchers will agree about validity. *Qualitative Health Research, 11*(4), 538–552.

Temple, B., & Young, A. (2004). Qualitative research and translation dilemmas. *Qualitative Research, 4*(2), 161–178.

Thompson, C., McCaughan, D., Cullum, N., Sheldon, T. A., & Raynor, P. (2004). Increasing the visibility of coding decisions in team-based qualitative research in nursing. *International Journal of Nursing Studies, 41*(1), 15–20.

Tobin, G. A., & Begley, C. M. (2004). Methodological rigour within a qualitative framework. *Journal of Advanced Nursing, 48*(4), 388–396.

Tracy, S. J. (2010). Qualitative quality: Eight "Big-Tent" criteria for excellent qualitative research. *Qualitative Inquiry, 16*, 837–851.

Waterman, H. (1998). Embracing ambiguities and valuing ourselves: Issues of validity in action research. *Journal of Advanced Nursing, 28*(1), 101–105.

Whittemore R., Chase, S. K., & Mandle, C. L. (2001). Validity in qualitative research. *Qualitative Health Research, 11*(4), 522–537.

Part III

Qualitative Synthesis as Evidence for Social Work Practice and Policy

8

Reporting Systematic
Qualitative Synthesis

ORGANIZING AND PRESENTING THE EVIDENCE

Transparency of the review process, a hallmark of qualitative synthesis that allows others to assess the review's quality and rigor, acts as a driving principle when considering how to organize and present the results of qualitative synthesis within systematic reviews. In this chapter, we illustrate strategies for detailing the organizing principles and techniques for reporting systematic qualitative synthesis. Findings in a systematic review approach should detail a clear process of the review and contextualize the presentation of the evidence to inform those who may want to use the findings. Moreover, a comprehensive presentation of the review means keeping detailed and accurate records throughout the review process (Pope, Mays, & Popay, 2007). *Record keeping* means recording: (a) all decision points made during the review, (b) a list of key questions for the review, (c) a list of search terms used, (d) the time period for conducting the search, (e) the number of hits located, (f) a detailed listing of the screening process and decisions to include or exclude studies, (g) the list of included studies, and (h) clear articulation of the steps taken for the data analysis and report writing.

DOCUMENTING THE SEARCH STRATEGY

To be transparent and systematic in the information-retrieval process, it is important that all search activities (e.g., search terms used, databases searched, journals hand searched, personal contacts) are documented in such detail that others know exactly the steps taken and can replicate them. For electronic searches, we developed a systematic information retrieval coding (see appendix A) to record each search for the review and to log results for each database and all gray literature searched. The systematic information-retrieval coding records: (a) the date(s) of the search, (b) the name of the researcher completing the search, (c) the database used for the search, (d) the specific search terms used in combination (including limiters and expanders), and (e) the number of results for each search strategy. The purpose of the systematic information-retrieval coding is to allow for replication. Furthermore, this level of detail enables the reviewer to save, copy, and paste the search strategy into the review, avoiding translation errors. To document the search strategy, it is important to use charts (see Figure 8.1) to show the various decision points and the resulting number of included and excluded studies at each of these decision points.

DESCRIBING THE INCLUDED AND EXCLUDED STUDIES

Included studies should be described in both chart and table formats so that the reader has a quick description of the studies. Columns in the tables of included studies should record the following for each study: the author, year of publication, study objectives, theoretical lens, sample recruitment, sample composition and size, location of sample, methodology, main results, strengths and limitations, and implications for practice and/or policy. These headings may change depending on the focus and purpose of the review. The purpose of the table is to provide the range of volume and range of evidence covered by the included studies in the review (Pope et al., 2007). Also important is to indicate which studies were excluded from the review process and to provide a detailed description of the reasons for the exclusion.

Illustrating the Recording Process: The FGDM Case

In our case illustration, a combination of completing a comprehensive search and revisiting gray literature searches resulted in the selection of

15 qualitative studies relevant to FGDM. By placing the included studies in table format (see Table 8.1), it became quickly apparent that most qualitative studies had been conducted in the United States, the United Kingdom, and New Zealand. A variety of methods were used in the primary studies including grounded theory ($n = 6$), Husserlian phenomenological approach ($n = 1$), case study analysis ($n = 1$), theme-based qualitative analysis ($n = 3$), qualitative summary of interviews ($n = 1$),

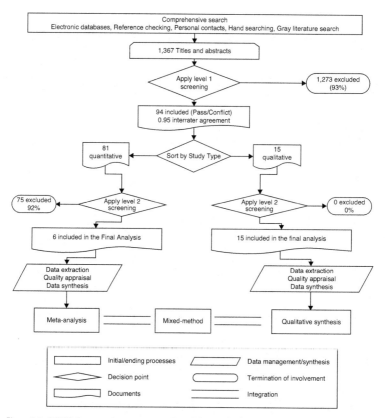

Figure 8.1 FGDM screening process. Graphic symbols are adapted from Practice network: I-O psychology. com-the internet and I-O psychology by M. M. Harris, 1999, *The Industrial-Organizational Psychologist, 36*, 89–93; copyright 1999 by American Psychology Association;) and *Handbook for synthesizing qualitative research* by M. Sandelowski and J. Barroso, 2007; copyright 2007 by Springer.

Table 8.1 Included FGDM Qualitative Studies

Study	Purpose	Location	Qualitative Approach	Sample	Data Analysis
Barrera (2006)	Focused on the relationship between family involvement in a structured therapeutic family intervention and the reduction of risk to the children	USA	Qualitative analytic strategy/ content analysis	20 child-protection workers	Retrospective interviews with child protection workers on their opinions of families to reduce risk to children
Bell (1996)	To evaluate the effects of involving families involved in FGDM	UK	Qualitative summary of interviews	40 mothers 23 fathers 8 children/ youth	Retrospective interviews with parents and children 1 to 4 weeks after participating in FGDM
Bell & Wilson (2006)	To explore the experiences of families who participated in FGDM	UK	Theme-based qualitative analysis	19 child-protection workers 35 family members 9 children/ youth	Retrospective interviews and surveys of workers with parents and children 6 weeks after participating in FGDM
Brodie (2008)	Examined the internal agency factors promoting and inhibiting family group conferencing and the reasons for the program's discontinuation after 8 years of operation	USA	Grounded theory	7 child-protection workers	In-depth interviews were conducted with 7 staff members

Brown (2007)	3 exploratory case study sites selected to explore the factors affecting implementation of the model in practice	UK	Case study analysis	Managers, senior managers, and social workers	Retrospective semistructured interviews
Connolly (2004)	To explore dynamics within FGDM in terms of both process and outcomes	New Zealand	Grounded theory	10 coordinators	Qualitative interviews with care and protection coordinators who had been convening conferences
Connolly (2006)	To explore experiences of coordinating conferences and changes in practice over time	New Zealand	Grounded theory	10 coordinators	Focus groups involved a guided discussion by the author
Crea & Berzin (2008)	To explore the level of support expressed by senior administrators as well as evidence of the allocation of sufficient resources and support from frontline staff	USA	Qualitative summary of interviews	89 agency staff members, legal professionals, and community partners	Interviews and focus groups were conducted to capture the unique characteristics of implementation

(Continued)

Table 8.1 Included FGDM Qualitative Studies (Continued)

Study	Purpose	Location	Qualitative Approach	Sample	Data Analysis
Dawson & Yancey (2006)	To share youth comments, based on their experience of FGDM	USA	Theme-based qualitative analysis	21 children/youth	Retrospective in-person interviews were conducted between 3 months and 1 year after FGDM
Gallagher & Jasper (2003)	To identify good practice, recognizing the challenges of the approach and enabling recommendations for improved collaboration to be framed	UK	Husserlian phenomenological approach	4 health visitors	Semistructured interviews using phenomenological analysis
Holland & O'Neil (2006)	To explore the views of children who have experienced an intervention designed to empower both them and their wider families	UK	Grounded theory	13 social workers 3 coordinators 31 family members 25 children/youth	Retrospective in-depth interviews 1 month after participating
Holland & Rivett (2008)	To examine the process of FGDM involving children and youth	UK	Grounded theory	25 children/youth	Retrospective semistructured interviews, analysis of documents, and collection of data on welfare outcomes. Children were reinterviewed after 6 months

Author (Year)	Aim	Country	Analysis	Sample	Description
Laws & Kirby (2007)	To study the best ways children and parents can take part in FGDM	USA	Theme-based qualitative analysis	20 parents 37 children/youth	Retrospective consultation interviews with parents and children who had taken part in FGDM
McCready & Donnelly (2005)	The identification of key strengths and challenges of implementing FGDM	USA	Theme-based qualitative analysis	15 parents 10 children/youth	Retrospective consultation interviews with parents and children who had taken part in FGDM
Neff (2006)	To explore process outcomes of FGDM	USA	Grounded theory	9 parents	Mixed-method comparison between child-protection clients in Hawaii receiving FGDM and child-protective services clients who had service plans developed using traditional means. Qualitative design included structured qualitative inquiry

and qualitative analytic strategy/content analysis ($n = 1$). Identifying the various methods included in the primary studies helped to plan which review method would be the most consistent with the goals and purposes of the qualitative synthesis.

A table of included studies can provide an overview of the scope of the findings. In the FGDM example, data in the table suggested that a range of participants have been included in the qualitative studies relevant to FGDM, including children, parents (mothers and fathers), child-protection workers, health visitors, coordinators, and agency staff. Depending on the goals of the review, decisions need to be made whether to focus the review on one group of participants (e.g., the children), on groupings of participants (children and parents), or to include all participant groups in the analysis.

DATA SYNTHESIS

Procedures for data analysis should be consistent with the chosen method for qualitative synthesis and should clearly distinguish the rationale, purpose, and process of the selected method used for data analysis. If the synthesis includes only qualitative studies, the data analysis strategy should distinguish among aggregating results, integrating the original meaning of the primary studies and reconstructing the findings into new interpretations of the data. In systematic reviews that include both qualitative and quantitative primary studies, the data analysis strategy should clearly report on the process of synthesizing quantitative and qualitative data within the review. Although methods for data analysis have been proposed for mixing and combining the results of both quantitative and qualitative data, we argue that separating the data analysis according to the type of studies included provides the most transparent method for detailing the specific analytical approaches.

REPORTING RESULTS

Depending on the method used for the qualitative synthesis, there are a range of options for reporting the results of the synthesis. Pope et al. (2007), for example, suggest that concept maps can be powerful visual tools to display concepts or categories of interest. Concept mapping includes multiple extracted evidence across studies to construct a model that highlights the key concepts relevant to the review question and it displays a relationship among the concepts identified (Pope et al., 2007). Concept maps can be handwritten or can be produced using brainstorm shapes, such as those produced in Microsoft Visio (Redmond, Washington). Figure 8.2, for example, maps the various concepts related to family engagement within the FGDM intervention based on the studies reviewed. In this example, the major concept of parent engagement is surrounded by minor concepts of voice, dynamics, climate, time, process, views, and plan. Each of these minor concepts have additional concepts connected to them that provide further insight into the barriers and facilitators of parent engagement as experienced by parents and children.

Key insights from the primary studies can also be displayed in table format so that broad conceptual comparisons can be made across studies (Pope et al., 2007). Depending on the complexity of these comparisons, these matrices can increase in complexity to demonstrate the various

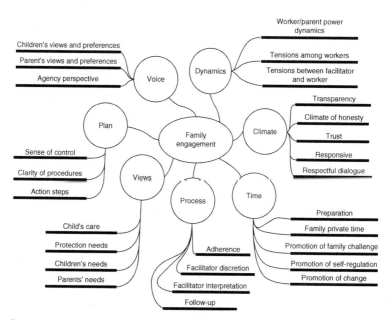

Figure 8.2 Concept Map of FGDM for Family Engagement.

connections among primary studies and to highlight differences between them. Table 8.2, for example, displays some of the benefits and risks of including children in FGDMs, as identified in the qualitative studies we reviewed.

Although charts, maps, and tables have the potential to oversimplify the complexity of the synthesis, nevertheless, they are useful for displaying final results. The use of specific charts, maps, or tables should also depend on the method used for the synthesis. For example, a line-of-argument graph is best to display a synthesis for a meta-ethnography study; vote counting is most consistent with meta-summary, as it provides an aggregative approach for tabulating the findings; though this

Table 8.2 Concept of Child Inclusion in FGDM (Truncated)

Source	Theoretical Assumptions	Benefits of Child Inclusion	Risks of Child Inclusion
Bell & Wilson (2006)	Child's right to participate	FGDM provides a valuable and valued resource	Children can feel confused after attending the intervention
Holland & O'Neill (2006)	The notion of empowerment of children and young people	Children can have positive experiences based on their participation in the family meetings. The families can feel a sense of "togetherness" once they reach a plan	The risk that children or young people will not be heard; they may feel that they are not being listened to, or that their participation is tokenistic; and they may be exposed to existing family conflict during the conference
Holland & Rivett (2008)	The therapeutic and emotional aspects of the FGC	FGCs can have strong emotional elements during the meeting process, and these may prompt positive change	Children may not experience the expression of raw emotion as helpful

approach is not methodologically sound for quantitative meta-analyses, meta-narrative approaches may best be displayed using complex interactions among concepts; and grounded theory formats may best be displayed using a matrix map of the interrelationships among concepts.

THE DISCUSSION

The focus of the discussion should be to explain how results answer each of the research questions identified and any new findings that emerge from the process of conducting the systematic review. When discussing the results of the qualitative synthesis, it is particularly important to focus on the context of the included studies to address issues of applicability and transferability. A discussion of the results should also be complimented by integrating what is already known about the research questions and comparing and contrasting the results with this evidence. Given the difficulty of writing the discussion in a coherent style, it may be useful to structure this section using subheadings to address the major points (Pope et al., 2007).

The discussion should include key messages based on the major findings of the review that can be summarized in a couple of sentences for each key message. The strengths and weaknesses of the findings should be discussed by exploring the population included in the primary reviews, the location of the studies, the inclusion of participants, the methods used in the primary studies, the sample characteristics, and the overall quality of the studies. Strengths and weaknesses of the systematic review should also be reported so as not to overemphasize the evidence and to discuss limitations of applicability and relevance based on the procedures used in the review process. Limitations can include language bias when only including English-language publications, publication bias when not including unpublished reports, selection bias when failing to be comprehensive in the information-retrieval strategy, and bias due to missing information and poor reporting in the primary studies. It is important to remember that all studies have limitations. The key is to articulate where and how substantial known biases may be influencing findings. If conclusions cannot be drawn due to these biases or other difficulties with the synthesis, then this should be clearly articulated in the discussion. Further, conclusions that are not drawn from the evidence should be clearly identified as such. Potential implications for social work practice and policy should be presented with caution and should avoid recommendations that are not supported from the evidence. Lastly, full disclosure of funding and conflicts of interest should be identified in the discussion and these should clearly be linked to potential bias of reporting and interpreting the findings.

DISSEMINATION OF RESULTS

As policy makers, service providers, and service users continue to demand the best available evidence, recent attention has turned toward developing models to best address the flow of information among these various stakeholders. There is growing concern that traditional strategies of dissemination of new evidence, which mainly involve journal publications and professional conferences, have limited influence on policy formation or services offered and delivered (Bate & Robert, 2002; Waddell et al., 2005). As the accessibility to information regarding issues and problems effecting consumers of knowledge increases, knowledge transfer and exchange has emerged as a potential conduit for translating evidence and fostering a more effective flow of knowledge to consumers (Tugwell, Robinson, Grimshaw & Santesso, 2006).

Knowledge transfer and exchange is a two-way process between researchers and stakeholders (Graham et al., 2006), which include clients, researchers, journal editors, commission and funding organizations, guideline developers, international synthesis collaborations (e.g., Cochrane Collaboration, Campbell Collaboration), evidence-based practice centers (Joanna Briggs Initiative, EPPI-Centre, EVIPNET centers) (Grimshaw et al., 2004). Grimshaw et al. (2004) state that knowledge translation and exchange should ensure both that research findings are brought to the attention of stakeholders and that the production of research is informed by the needs of all stakeholders. To increase the utility of knowledge creation based on systematic reviews for stakeholders, Grimshaw et al. (2004) suggest five key questions that should be explored: To whom should research knowledge be transferred? What should be transferred? With what effect should research knowledge be transferred? By whom should research knowledge be transferred? How should research knowledge be transferred?

Knowledge transfer and exchange fit well with the strengths-based, patient-/client-centered approaches of both policy and service delivery. This is particularly true because such models can empower people to be critical consumers of knowledge, thereby affording them greater control over decisions relating to their well-being. As users are becoming more sophisticated at stating their needs and making progressive steps through new methods of networking and communication, they are increasingly better able to reach consensus on those needs and to articulate them. As better consumers of research, stakeholders take on a greater role in exploring the transferability and applicability of the new knowledge gained from the results of qualitative systematic reviews. By ensuring a transparent approach for knowledge transfer and exchange, results of systematic qualitative synthesis are put into the hands of stakeholders to assess both credibility and relevance of findings. It can also help to ensure that research has maximum impact; strengthen the relevance of research; provide a direct link to consumers; and facilitate a multidisciplinary approach to the creation, dissemination, and evaluation of knowledge. In short, knowledge transfer and exchange is a central component of systematic qualitative synthesis because the process goes far beyond traditional knowledge dissemination practices in providing the tools necessary for consumers to explore the transferability of knowledge produced by qualitative synthesis reviews.

KEY POINTS TO REMEMBER

- Transparency of the review process allows others to assess the review's quality and rigor and to explore the transferability of the knowledge produced by the qualitative synthesis.
- Transparency is also the key process for assessing the transferability and applicability of knowledge produced by the qualitative synthesis.
- A comprehensive and transparent presentation of the review process means keeping detailed and accurate records throughout the project (Pope et al., 2007).
- Results should be displayed in several ways including topical tables and concept maps.
- Findings should be grouped by method, linking back to the question(s) posed in the protocol.

- Knowledge transfer and exchange is a two-way process for ensuring qualitative syntheses have maximum impact and for attempting to meet the needs of stakeholders.
- Knowledge transfer and exchange helps to facilitate a multidisciplinary approach to the creation, dissemination, and evaluation of knowledge.

SUGGESTED READING

Computer Assisted Qualitative Data Analysis Software

Banner, D. J., & Albarrran, J. W. (2009). Computer-assisted qualitative data analysis software: A review. *Canadian Journal of Cardiovascular Nursing*, *19*(3), 24–31.

Creswell, J. W., & Maietta, R. (2002). Qualitative data analysis software. In D. C. Miller & N. J. Salkind (Eds.), *Handbook of research design and social measurement* (6th ed., pp. 143–200). Thousand Oaks, CA: Sage Publications.

Drisko, J. W. (2004). Qualitative data analysis software: A user's appraisal. In D. Padgett (Ed.), *The qualitative research experience* (rev. ed., pp. 193–209). Belmont, CA: Wadsworth.

Lewins, A. (2008). CAQDAS: Computer assisted qualitative data analysis. In N. Gielbert (Ed.), *Researching social life* (3rd ed., pp. 343–357). London: Sage Publications.

Lewins, A., & Silver, C. (2007). *Using software in qualitative research: A step-by-step guide.* London: Sage Publications.

Lewis, R. B. (2004). NVivo 2.0 and ATLAS.ti 5.0: A comparative review of two popular qualitative data-analysis programs. *Field Methods, 16*(4), 439–464.

Silver, C., & Fielding, N. (2008). Using computer assisted qualitative data analysis. In C. Willing & W. Stainton-Rogers (Eds.), *The Sage handbook of qualitative research in psychology* (pp.). London: Sage Publications.

9

Future Directions for Social Work Practice and Policy

Qualitative knowledge is absolutely essential as a prerequisite foundation for quantification in any science. Without competence at the qualitative level, one's computer printout is misleading or meaningless. We failed in our thinking about programme evaluation methods to emphasize the need for a qualitative context.... To rule out plausible hypotheses we need situation specific wisdom. The lack of this knowledge (whether it be called ethnography or program history or gossip) makes us incompetent estimators of programme impacts, turning out conclusions that are not only wrong, but often wrong in socially destructive ways.

—(Campbell, 1984, p. 36)

SYSTEMATIC REVIEWS IN SOCIAL WORK

Social work is a relatively late adopter of systematic review methods. The Campbell Collaboration, whose current mission is to help people "make well-informed decisions by preparing, maintaining and disseminating systematic reviews in education, crime and justice, and social welfare" (www.campbellcollaboration.org), has made an important contribution to the social work field in promoting, developing, and providing guidance in conducting social work–related reviews during the past decade. In other arenas as well, there is a growing emphasis on the role of systematic reviews for social work research, practice, and policy (e.g., Littell, Corcoran, & Pallai, 2008), and it is expected that systematic reviews will continue to play an important role in evidence-based practice in social work.

QUALITATIVE SYNTHESIS WITHIN THE EBP MOVEMENT

As the number of publications increases, social workers will be less able to keep up with the literature, even within specific areas of practice and policy. In addition, the large volume of research also presents challenges in terms of establishing the quality of such studies and how to contend with contradictory results. Systematic reviews have emerged as one of the most important tools for successfully conducting the process of EBP, providing comprehensive and transparent summaries of the research on a single question of relevance. These reviews use thorough and systematic search methods to bring together large numbers of individual studies in a single document, providing a clear appraisal of the literature in a straightforward manner.

To date, systematic reviews have largely focused on quantitative research, mostly related to examining the efficacy and effectiveness of specific interventions. Similar to the health sciences (Popay, 2006), this has created an underutilization of accumulated qualitative studies that have the potential to inform, enhance, extend, and supplement quantitative methods for conducting systematic reviews. We would argue that quantitative outcome measures, though clearly important, tend to be fairly crude in terms of providing an understanding of how clients experience their problems, successes, and their interactions with social workers and other helping professionals. Often, the story is in the person and in the contexts in which people interact, and we have not yet seen any randomized controlled trials that speak to the lived experience of clients! Indeed, as we have proposed throughout, the systematic review process is a fruitful means of tapping into and harnessing this potential treasure trove of valuable insights into people's experiences and into the meanings of activities and events articulated within the sociocultural context being considered (Valadez & Bamberger, 1994). The purpose of a systematic synthesis of qualitative research is not to reach a singular "truth" in regards to the evidence. Rather, it is designed to provide a more comprehensive understanding of the range of client and professional experiences, contexts, and events, including commonalities and differences. Many times, these will be in the context of a social work intervention.

Importantly, we emphasize the necessity of exacting a fit between the research question and the corresponding method—whether it is qualitative or quantitative. This is crucial both for individual studies and for systematic reviews. For example, the difficulties in conducting quantitative research to investigate complex phenomenon, such as community initiatives within marginalized populations, might suggest that qualitative approaches would be the more relevant method to answer such detailed and multifaceted questions. However, qualitative methods are not well-suited, on their own for exploring the effectiveness of large-scale interventions because of their unique focus on depth, rather than breadth, of understanding. Additionally, the suitability of using qualitative research to identify causal mechanisms remains controversial and underdeveloped (Johnson & Onwuegbuzie, 2004; Smith, 1995). The movement toward having individual practitioners and organizations conduct finely honed searches of the literature, an essential component of the process of EBP, requires that all evidence be considered and, where applicable, used. Qualitative research is surely an important part of the evidence base in terms of context about clients and the interventions themselves. The difficulty comes with trying to synthesize an often fragmented and incomplete body of literature, and we would argue that systematic reviews offer the most honest, transparent, and rigorous summaries of evidence for use in social work practice and policy.

MORE SEAMLESS INTEGRATION OF QUALITATIVE STUDIES WITH QUANTITATIVE SYSTEMATIC REVIEWS

Mixed-method research designs have been more popular in other disciplines, including nursing (Sandelowski, 2001), education (Johnson & Onwuegbuzie, 2004,), health sciences (Morgan, 1998), and program evaluation (Green, Caracelli, & Graham, 1989). In social work, mixed-method designs have a controversial history, possibly—because of the challenges of mixing methods from different epistemological worldviews (e.g., post-positivism and interpretivism). We concur with Padgett's (2008) suggestion that mixed-method research is particularly relevant to social work because the profession is interested in effective outcomes for clients while also wanting to understand their lived experiences. Mixed-method can also provide fruitful information about how these outcomes are perceived by others and about the potential social barriers and facilitators that may influence clients from achieving these desired outcomes. Although many social workers support the multimethod approach (Davis, 1994; Glisson, 1990; Grinnell, 1997; Harrison, 1994; Padgett, 2004, 2008), strong examples specific to social work are only now beginning to emerge.

Mixed-method approaches provide greater confidence in a singular conclusion, and interpretations and conclusions can be modified by information from both approaches. The rationale for the mixed-method approach is not to simply corroborate findings but rather to expand our understanding. Mixed-method designs can help to identify overlapping and emerging features discovered from an initial method and can help to identify contradictions found from multiple sources (Greene et al., 1989). Mixed-method studies may also be generative, as inconsistencies and contradictions are engaged and "fresh insights, new perspectives, and original understandings" emerge (Greene, 2007, p. 103).

Although the Cochrane Qualitative Research Methods Group (Higgins & Green, 2008, chapter 20) has developed guidelines for integrating qualitative research with randomized trials, no such guidance currently exists for integrating randomized controlled trials in qualitative systematic reviews nor for how to complete systematic reviews limited to qualitative studies. Nonetheless, the value of integrating evidence from multiple types of studies in systematic reviews is increasingly recognized (Thomas et al., 2004). As we have argued, qualitative synthesis can complement quantitative reviews by helping to define and refine the question, thus allowing for maximum relevance and for synthesizing evidence from qualitative research identified while looking for evidence of effectiveness. Qualitative synthesis can also address questions other than those related to effectiveness (Popay, 2006).

Key topics of interest to social work recently addressed in published syntheses of qualitative research include:

- Parenting programmes: A systematic review and synthesis of qualitative research (Kane, Wood, & Barlow, 2007)
- Homeless adolescent mothers: A metasynthesis of their life experiences (Meadows-Oliver, 2006)

- Cancer and disability benefits: A synthesis of qualitative findings on advice and support (Wilson & Amir, 2008)
- The essence of healing from sexual violence: A qualitative metasynthesis (Draucker et al., 2009)
- Understanding Australian rural women's ways of achieving health and wellbeing: A metasynthesis of the literature (Harvey, 2007)
- Anorexia nervosa's meaning to patients: A qualitative synthesis (Espíndola & Blay, 2009)
- Using qualitative assessment and review instrument software to synthesise studies on older people's views and experiences of falls prevention (McInnes & Wimpenny, (2008)
- Patients' help-seeking experiences and delay in cancer presentation: A qualitative synthesis (Smith, Pope, & Botha, 2005).

As the interest in systematic synthesis gains traction, we expect that the field will begin to embrace different methods for mixing and integrating quantitative and qualitative primary studies in systematic reviews, and that we will see this area of research advance and achieve greater sophistication.

REGISTRY OF QUALITATIVE STUDIES WITHIN INTERVENTION RESEARCH

Because of the lack of consensus about which systematic review methods for integrating qualitative and quantitative studies should be adopted, the majority of qualitative syntheses within systematic reviews are currently not being registered with the Cochrane or Campbell Libraries. Systematic reviews that combine qualitative and quantitative studies have been published in a number of different journals and across a number of disciplines. To further enhance the development of methods for conducting qualitative synthesis within systematic reviews, a registry should be created so that there is a central place to compare and contrast the various approaches. In fact, a major new line of inquiry might be developed that compares these methods, articulating which approaches are best suited to the various questions, contexts, and populations of interest found in social work.

MORE AGREEMENT ON FRAMEWORK FOR SYNTHESIS

Qualitative research is increasingly valued as part of the evidence for social work policy and practice, but the methods used for conducting qualitative synthesis of this evidence are still being contested. Although the area is developing rapidly, there remain many methodological challenges to consider. Our ideas about qualitative synthesis within systematic reviews will not resolve these debates. Our hope is that our efforts will be helpful in the exploration of the various decision points that still need to be debated and decided upon in the future.

CONCLUDING REMARKS: A WAY FORWARD

Social workers can and should avail themselves of the findings from systematic syntheses, and they can also participate in all stages of the development and implementation of systematic syntheses and the broader family of systematic reviews. Knowledge creation involves the acquisition of accumulated evidence and expertise to gain new insights on a particular problem, issue, or event. When multiple sources of knowledge exist for a particular problem, the accumulation of existing knowledge should involve explicit, systematic, and reproducible methods to identify, appraise, and synthesize studies relevant to a specific question. Systematic synthesis of knowledge can then lead to clear, concise, and explicit evidence to meet informational needs with practical guidelines and recommendations.

Social workers can participate in identifying questions that are clinically and policy-relevant to address gaps in knowledge relevant to current social work practice and policy. Problem formulation refers to the identification of the kinds of knowledge consumers need and the identification of gaps in this knowledge that could otherwise inform, educate, and change attitudes and/or behaviors. Social workers can initiate the knowledge development process by leading the identification, review, and selection of existing information needed to address the problem.

Social workers can also participate in researcher–practitioner teams to develop methodological protocols for answering complex phenomena involving different strategies (e.g., meta-analytic designs to answer effectiveness-based questions and qualitative synthesis to explore participant views and preferences). Although qualitative studies are not produced with the intention to direct clinical or policy changes, the emphasis on the rich context-sensitive experiences within these studies have important implications for generating a better understanding of the context of clinical social work and its governing policies.

Social workers can also be involved with systematic review teams to locate potentially relevant resources to be included in syntheses and/or quantitative reviews. Taking part in the retrieval, screening, and synthesis of qualitative studies are important ways that social workers can use their expertise to ensure that the information-retrieval strategies used are relevant to the social work context. Searches for studies involving complex interventions can be complicated, requiring a more comprehensive approach. If too broad, searches can produce information overload and can slow down the systematic review process. Conversely, overly simplistic strategies can compromise the review by missing critical studies relevant to the reviews' stated question(s). Finding the balance of sensitivity and specificity is further strained by the unique complexity of interventions, especially those in the social sciences. For these reviews, conventional information-retrieval strategies should be complemented with additional social science search techniques to locate high quality references (Hammerstrøm, Wade, & Klint Jørgensen, 2010).

Social workers with experience of working with qualitative data and using different methods are especially needed to ensure that the synthesis process is congruent and consistent with practice in order to facilitate the transferability of findings. They can also participate in user groups and advisory committees to provide research teams with guidance in terms of the relevance of specific systematic review questions for social work practice and policy. Although knowledge transfer evolved through attempts to extend the impact of research through dissemination, there is a shift in knowledge mobilization whereby such research partnerships are encouraged in order to better integrate research with the needs of policy makers and service providers (Gollop, et al., 2006; Léveillé, Trocmé, Chamberland, & Brown, 2011).

Finally, as informed consumers of systematic reviews, social workers can play an important role in the translation of findings from systematic reviews to various stakeholders. Being included as an active part of the research enterprise requires that social workers keep up to date on the literature in their given area and use the collective knowledge garnered by reviews in areas that influence the work they do with clients. As a result, they may be less likely to be deceived by poorly conducted research, and they can be more secure in the knowledge that guides their work.

Knowledge based on the accumulation of qualitative studies is predicated on finding better ways to integrate these qualitative stories, rather than letting them simply accumulate in academic journals. Despite the epistemological and ontological challenges inherent in weaving these stories together, efforts to develop methods for qualitative synthesis can enhance our collective wisdom and make for more relevant social work practice and policy. Although it is clear that the techniques of qualitative synthesis remain underdeveloped and are in need of further exploration, we are optimistic that current qualitative methods for synthesis and future work in this area will enhance our collective knowledge and, ultimately, improve the ways in which we carry out our duties as critically informed helping professionals.

The contribution of social work to the development and refinement of systematic reviews of qualitative research is invaluable given social work's focus on both the effectiveness of its interventions and the lived experiences of the people we serve. In a very real sense, social workers are uniquely positioned to advance the evidence needed for effective services while advocating for client participation in the knowledge creation activities that affect them.

KEY POINTS TO REMEMBER

- Similar to other methods for systematic reviews, we present a comprehensive and transparent approach for "locating and synthesizing research that bears on a particular question, using organized, transparent, and replicable procedures at each step in the process" (Littell et al., 2008, p. 1).
- Presenting the synthesis of qualitative studies within the family of systematic reviews moves qualitative synthesis out of the shadow of quantitative systematic reviews and meta-analyses.
- Systematic synthesis of qualitative studies offers a transparent and systematic process to capture accumulated qualitative evidence.
- Evidence derived from qualitative research can complement outcome studies by providing critical information about results found.

- Combining quantitative with qualitative studies in this way provides researchers with important information about how and why the interventions worked, as well as how and why they substantially altered the findings of the larger quantitative study.
- Systematic synthesis of qualitative research meets an urgent need for social work researchers to find ways to appropriately use knowledge derived from qualitative studies to inform social work policy and practice.
- Despite the contingent nature of evidence gleaned from synthesis of qualitative studies and a current lack of consensus about the veracity of some of its aspects, systematic synthesis is an important technique and, used suitably, can deepen our understanding of the contextual dimensions of social work practice.
- We have outlined a range of methods and strategies for synthesizing qualitative research findings. We have attempted to select examples relevant to social work to illustrate these methods. These examples will hopefully inspire others to consider questions relevant to social work to help build our collective understanding of the various ways that systematic synthesis of qualitative research can help inform practice, research, and policy decisions. This is a growing area of research in social work, and we expect that the use of systematic syntheses in social work will continue to increase.
- The contribution of social work to the development and refinement of systematic reviews of qualitative research is invaluable given social work's focus on both the effectiveness of its interventions and the lived experiences of the people we serve.
- In a very real sense, social workers are uniquely positioned to advance the evidence needed for effective services while advocating for client participation in knowledge creation activities that affect them.

SUGGESTED READING

Atkins, D. (2007). Creating and synthesizing evidence with decision makers in mind: Integrating evidence from clinical trials and other study designs. *Medical Care, 45*, S16–S22.

Barbour, R. S. (2003). The newfound credibility of qualitative research? Tales of technical essentialism and co-option. *Qualitative Health Research, 13*(7), 1019–1027.

Beck, C. (2003). Seeing the forest for the trees: A qualitative synthesis project. *Journal of Nursing Education, 42,* 318–323.

Creswell, J. W. (2003). *Research design: Qualitative, quantitative, and mixed methods approaches* (2nd ed.). Thousand Oaks, CA: Sage.

Finfgeld, D. L. (2003). Meta-synthesis: The state of the art—so far. *Qualitative Health Research, 13*(7), 893–904.

Flemming, K. (2007). Research methodologies. Synthesis of qualitative research and evidenced-based nursing. *British Journal of Nursing, 16,* 616–620.

Greene, J. C., & Caracelli, V. J. (Eds.). (1997). *Advances in mixed-method evaluation: The challenges and benefits of integrated diverse paradigms.* San Francisco: Jossey-Bass.

Kaplan, B., & Duchon, D. (1988). Combining qualitative and quantitative approaches in information systems research: A case study. *Management Information Systems Quarterly, 12*(4), 571–584.

Morgan, D. (1998). Practical strategies for combining qualitative and quantitative methods: Applications to health research. *Qualitative Health Research, 8*(3), 362–376.

Morse, J. (2006). The politics of evidence. *Qualitative Health Research, 16,* 395–404.

Newman, I., & Benz, C. R. (1998). *Qualitative-quantitative research methodology: Exploring the interactive continuum.* Carbondale: Southern Illinois University Press.

Sayer, A. (1992). *Method in social science: A realist approach* (2nd ed.). London: Routledge.

Steckler, A., McLeroy, K. R., Goodman, R. M., Bird, S. T., & McCormick, L. (1992). Toward integrating qualitative and quantitative methods: An introduction. *Health Education Quarterly, 19*(1), 1–8,

Tashakkori, A., & Teddlie, C. (2003). *Handbook of mixed methods in the social and behavioral sciences.* Thousand Oaks, CA: Sage.

Appendix A

Systematic Information Retrieval Coding Sheet

Project: _____

Reviewer: _____

Date(s) of Search: _____

Search Method:

Electronic Databases

- Psychological Abstracts (PsycInfo, PsycLIT, ClinPsyc-*clinical subset*)
- MEDLINE
- EMBASE
- Database of Reviews of Effectiveness (DARE online)
- ChildData (child health and welfare)
- ASSIA (applied social sciences)
- Caredata (social work)
- Social Work Abstracts
- Child Abuse, Child Welfare, & Adoption
- Cochrane Collaboration
- C2-SPECTR
- Social Sciences Abstracts
- Social Service Abstracts
- Dissertation Abstracts International (DAI)
- Other (depending on focus of the review)

Electronic Search Engines

- Biblioline
- Google

Hand-Searched Journals
(Journals are picked for being relevant to the research question)

Gray Literature
- Conference Proceedings: _____
- Research Reports:_____
- Government Reports:_____
- Book Chapters:_____
- Dissertations:_____
- Policy Documents:_____
- Personal Networks:_____
- Research Organizations' Web Sites:_____
Language(s): _____
Date Range: _____
Description of Search:
Search Terms (limiters and expanders are expressed in OVID terms and will be adjusted based on database searched)

Search Term Combinations (including all limiters and expanders)	Results

Appendix B

Qualitative Research Quality Checklist

Reference Review:
Reference Number:
Reviewer:
Date(s) of the Review:
Reference ID:
Author(s):
Year of Publication:
Title:
Location of Reference:
Source:
☐ Book
☐ Conference Paper
☐ Peer Reviewed Journal Article
☐ Non-Peer Reviewed Journal Article

☐ Dissertation
☐ Report
☐ Government Publication
☐ Other: _____

Search Method:
☐ Electronic Search:
☐ Hand Search:
☐ Gray Literature:
☐ Reference Check:
☐ Consultation:
☐ Other: _____

Qualitative Framework	Applicable	Addressed	Review Comments
1. Is the purpose and research question(s) stated clearly?	☐ Yes ☐ No ☐ Unclear	☐ Yes ☐ No ☐ Unclear	
2. Is a qualitative approach appropriate to answer the research question (e.g., exploratory vs. explanatory)?	☐ Yes ☐ No ☐ Unclear	☐ Yes ☐ No ☐ Unclear	

Study Setting	Applicable	Addressed	Review Comments
3. Is the setting of the study appropriate and specific for exploring the research question?	☐ Yes ☐ No ☐ Unclear	☐ Yes ☐ No ☐ Unclear	
4. Is there prolonged engagement to render the inquirer open to multiple influences?	☐ Yes ☐ No ☐ Unclear	☐ Yes ☐ No ☐ Unclear	
5. Is there persistent observation in the setting to focus on the issues relevant to the research question?	☐ Yes ☐ No ☐ Unclear	☐ Yes ☐ No ☐ Unclear	

Study Design	Applicable	Addressed	Review Comments
6. Is the research design appropriate for the research question?	☐ Yes ☐ No ☐ Unclear	☐ Yes ☐ No ☐ Unclear	

Sampling Procedures	Applicable	Addressed	Review Comments
7. Is the process of sample selection adequately described and consistent with the research design/ research question?	☐ Yes ☐ No ☐ Unclear	☐ Yes ☐ No ☐ Unclear	
8. Is the sample size and composition justified and appropriate for the research design/ research question?	☐ Yes ☐ No ☐ Unclear	☐ Yes ☐ No ☐ Unclear	

Data Collection	Applicable	Addressed	Review Comments
9. Are the methods for data collection adequately described?	☐ Yes ☐ No ☐ Unclear	☐ Yes ☐ No ☐ Unclear	

Data Collection	Applicable	Addressed	Review Comments
10. Are the methods for data collection consistent with the research question?	☐ Yes ☐ No ☐ Unclear	☐ Yes ☐ No ☐ Unclear	
11. Is a range of methods used for triangulation?	☐ Yes ☐ No ☐ Unclear	☐ Yes ☐ No ☐ Unclear	
12. Is there an articulation of who collected the data, when the data was collected and who analyzed the data?	☐ Yes ☐ No ☐ Unclear	☐ Yes ☐ No ☐ Unclear	
13. Is there an audit trail regarding data collection including tapes, memos, and note taking of decisions made in the study?	☐ Yes ☐ No ☐ Unclear	☐ Yes ☐ No ☐ Unclear	

Ethical Issues	Applicable	Addressed	Review Comments
14. Is there adequate consideration for ethical issues, such as informed consent, privacy, and confidentiality and protection from harm?	☐ Yes ☐ No ☐ Unclear	☐ Yes ☐ No ☐ Unclear	

Reflexivity of the Researcher	Applicable	Addressed	Review Comments
15. Has the researcher identified potential and actual biases (both as researcher and in the research design)?	☐ Yes ☐ No ☐ Unclear	☐ Yes ☐ No ☐ Unclear	

16. Did the researcher integrate the use of a reflexive journal in the data analysis and interpretation?	☐ Yes ☐ No ☐ Unclear	☐ Yes ☐ No ☐ Unclear	

Data Analysis	**Applicable**	**Addressed**	**Review Comments**
17. Is the process of data analysis presented with sufficient detail and depth to provide insight into the meanings and perceptions of the sample?	☐ Yes ☐ No ☐ Unclear	☐ Yes ☐ No ☐ Unclear	
18. Are quotes used to match concepts and themes derived from the raw data?	☐ Yes ☐ No ☐ Unclear	☐ Yes ☐ No ☐ Unclear	

Findings	**Applicable**	**Addressed**	**Review Comments**
19. Do the findings emerge from the experiences/ subjective interpretations of the sample?	☐ Yes ☐ No ☐ Unclear	☐ Yes ☐ No ☐ Unclear	
20. Was member checking employed?	☐ Yes ☐ No ☐ Unclear	☐ Yes ☐ No ☐ Unclear	
21. Does the researcher provide "thick description" of the sample and results to appraise transferability?	☐ Yes ☐ No ☐ Unclear	☐ Yes ☐ No ☐ Unclear	

Authenticity	**Applicable**	**Addressed**	**Review Comments**
22. Were stakeholders involved in the project?	☐ Yes ☐ No ☐ Unclear	☐ Yes ☐ No ☐ Unclear	

Fairness	**Applicable**	**Addressed**	**Review Comments**
23. Did all stakeholders have equal access to the research process and benefits?	☐ Yes ☐ No ☐ Unclear	☐ Yes ☐ No ☐ Unclear	

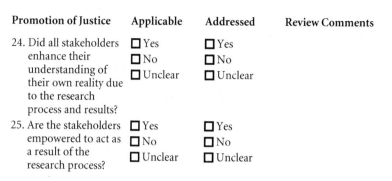

Promotion of Justice	Applicable	Addressed	Review Comments
24. Did all stakeholders enhance their understanding of their own reality due to the research process and results?	☐ Yes ☐ No ☐ Unclear	☐ Yes ☐ No ☐ Unclear	
25. Are the stakeholders empowered to act as a result of the research process?	☐ Yes ☐ No ☐ Unclear	☐ Yes ☐ No ☐ Unclear	

Overall Impressions:

BACKGROUND:

The Qualitative Research Quality Checklist (QRQC) was created based on existing research regarding the standards for measuring qualitative designs, as well as consultation with experts in the field of qualitative research. QRQC is a 25-point quality appraisal form designed to evaluate credibility, dependability, confirmability, transferability, authenticity, and relevance of qualitative studies.

QRQC appraises qualitative studies in terms of the epistemological and theoretical frameworks, study setting, study design, sampling procedures, data collection, ethical issues, reflexivity of the researcher, data analysis, and reporting of the findings. In addition, fairness and promotion of justice are included to evaluate studies where the central purpose is to empower participants through participant action research. Not all quality appraisal indicators will be relevant to a study because of differences in the epistemological and ontological stances taken by the investigators. For this reason, QRQC includes three columns for each quality appraisal item: The first column questions whether the quality domain is relevant to the particular study. The second column questions whether there is sufficient information in the study to suggest that it has been addressed in the specific domain of quality. The third column is an open comment box so the reviewer can make interpretive comments about the study and/or of the qualitative domain being assessed and its relevance.

Underlying Assumptions of QRQC

The emerging qualitative "story" matters, not the discrete ratings of quality. The underlying assumption of this critical appraisal tool is that, regardless of the epistemological or ontological assumptions guiding a particular qualitative study, the story should be told in a consistent, transparent way and should adhere to the highest standard of methods associated with the philosophical traditions the investigators purportedly draw from. The appraisal tool is not a means of excluding studies based on "quality," but it provides the opportunity to evaluate the quality of studies based on dimensions that have been agreed on by the scientific community.

Discretion, reflection, and flexibility remain central, and this provides "guideposts" for evaluating the quality of studies. As such, the interpretation of "quality" becomes part of the reviewer's interpretation of the studies. It is important to move away from the blind utilization of quality tools to justify credibility. At the same time, there is a need for further guidance on ways to assess quality and integrate these interpretations into the analysis. We propose that an interpretative tool with selected guideposts for quality may provide reviewers with the needed flexibility within common standards of quality.

Comments and Reflections

The QRQC form provides space for comments and reflections for each dimension as well as an "overall impressions" box. The purpose of these text boxes is to provide the reviewer with the opportunity to write commentaries and explanations of appraisal for each dimension and, at the end, to integrate these into an overall impression of quality. These narrative reflections are important when comparing the quality of multiple qualitative studies, and they can easily be incorporated into the text of the review.

Glossary

Action research A progressive process of problem-solving in large teams, organizations, or institutions led by individuals to address and improve specific issues, strategies, practices, and knowledge. Action researchers typically work with and for people rather than conduct research on them for increased knowledge and action.

Aggregative synthesis Involves techniques, such as meta-summary, that are concerned with assembling and pooling data.

Analyzing qualitative data (see also data analysis) Analysis of qualitative data is as an ongoing process that begins with the identification of the research questions and continues throughout the data collection process to the presentation of the findings.

Assessment of study quality Involves the assessment of quality based on the methodological soundness and rigor of primary studies.

Auditing or audit trail An independent third party reviews the interview guide, field notes, tapes, and transcripts and assesses the evidence of data reduction, analysis, and category construction.

Authenticity Involves a quality criterion to assess whether the interpretations and findings are genuine reflections of the participants' experiences.

Bayesian approaches to synthesis A graphic representation of random variables and their conditional independence represented through an acyclic graph.

Bibliographical databases May be a centralized location in which records, books, or other materials are held both electronically and in a library. Most bibliographic databases appear as indexes, which contain citations, abstracts, or full-texts of original articles.

Campbell Collaboration The Campbell Collaboration (C2) is a nonprofit organization that develops, approves, and distributes systematic reviews within social welfare, education, crime and justice, and international development.

Case studies A thorough examination of a single individual, family, group, organization, community, or society using all available evidence for that case.

Cochrane Collaboration The Cochrane Collaboration is a nonprofit organization of over ten thousand volunteers in over 90 countries worldwide who review the effects of healthcare interventions through randomized controlled trials and systematic reviews, which are published in the Cochrane Library.

Coding This is a technique in the analysis process. It is the process of conceptualizing the data derived from the text or created by the researcher to represent themes in the data.

Computer-assisted qualitative data analysis software (CAQDAS) The use of computer technology to code text, identify key phrases, perform content analysis, and retrieve coded sections of text. CAQDAS do not, however, replace interpretative analysis by the researcher.

Confirmability Concerned with establishing that the participants and the context of the enquiry rather than the biases, motivations, and perspectives of the researcher have determined the findings of a study.

Constructivist paradigm Considers that the socially constructed reality and participants construct reality in the mind from the world around them.

Content analysis A research method in which all forms of communication are transcribed and analyzed by coding and noting the frequency in the occurrence of certain content and themes.

Convenience or accidental sampling A sampling method that uses availability and convenience to find and recruit participants to the sample.

Credibility Refers to whether the study findings make sense and whether the findings are credible and meaningful to the participants of the research and to the readers.

Criteria The standard on which a judgment or decision can be based.

Critical appraisal A process of systematically examining research to establish its value and relevance to the larger research context.

Critical interpretive synthesis A construction of critical analysis of a complex body of literature.

Cross-study synthesis Used in qualitative method in which the researchers investigate other studies while maintaining their concentration on the themes derived in the primary study.

Data analysis The process of gathering, modeling, and transforming data by highlighting useful information, exploring current gaps in research, compiling conclusions, and offering recommendations for policy or further research.

Data collection methods (see individual entries for each method) Most common data collection methods in qualitative research include the use of interviews, focus groups, observations, case analysis, and analysis of artifacts (e.g., pictures, objects).

Data management, storage, and retrieval Data management uses computer storage, memory, components, devices, and media to aid in the organization, storage, and retrieval of data.

Delphi consensus analysis A systematic forecasting method performed by a panel of experts. The experts answer questions in rounds and a facilitator anonymously summarizes the rounds.

Dependability The extent that the findings of a study would be repeated if the enquiry were replicated with the same or similar participants in the same or a similar context.

Emergent design The use of a theoretical framework to conduct a study and to decide on a methodological design as new data and themes present themselves to the researcher.

Epistemology The study of knowledge that provides a philosophical grounding for knowledge creation and a rationale for belief.

Ethnography To describe and interpret a cultural and social group. It is a study of an intact cultural or social group based primarily on observations and a prolonged period of time spent by the researcher in the field.

Evidence-based practice An integration of individual practice expertise with the best available empirical evidence from systematic research and the values and expectations of clients.

Exclusion criteria (see also inclusion criteria) Reasons used to determine whether a study will be excluded in a research synthesis based on predetermined criteria, such as population, research design, intervention, and such.

Explanation Based on explanatory logic, different research design may aim to be comparative, developmental, descriptive, predictive, or theoretical.

Field studies A scientific study of specific groups or individuals in their natural environment.

Fieldwork A method of data collection in field research and being involved in the natural environment of that which is being studied.

Focus group A research technique in which a small group of people are brought together and guided through an interview and/or discussion on specific topics and ideas to capitalize on group interaction and communication to generate data.

Generalizability To make inferences that can be applied not only to the group being studied but also to the larger community of which that group belongs.

Gray literature Studies that have not been published in journals or other means and may be difficult to find through conventional means.

Grounded theory A qualitative approach used to describe the inductive process of identifying analytical themes or categories as they emerge from the data.

Hand searching A systematic and thorough process in which all articles of a journal or subject matter are hand searched and screened for their relevance to the topic being studied.

Heterogeneity A term used to describe a sample that consists of multiple aspects, elements, or variations within a group.

Homogeneity A term used to describe a sample that consists of similar aspects, elements, and minimal variation within the group.

Inclusion criteria (see also exclusion criteria) A set of conditions or standards that are set and need to be met in order to include a primary study within a research synthesis.

Interaction Considering how interaction between researcher and participants influences meaning and interpretation.

Interpretation To provide space for subjective meanings, perceptions, and experiences.

Interpretive paradigm Concerned with the internal reality of participants or the research subjects. The purpose is to explore the lives of participants in order to understand and interpret the meaning effectively.

Interpretive validity Seeks to capture the researchers' or readers' understanding of events, objects, and behaviors and if they will be correct in those assumptions.

Interview Typically one-to-one conversations to explore issues in detail; respondents are encouraged to reveal opinions, attitudes, and experiences.

Member check A process in qualitative research to engage participants in providing feedback to help researchers improve accuracy, credibility, and authenticity of the research interpretations and findings.

Memoing A method of writing down the researcher's thought process while engaged in the analysis process.

Meta-analysis The use of statistical techniques to combine the results of studies addressing the same question into a summary measure.

Meta-ethnography The qualitative synthesis method of extracting concepts, metaphors, and themes arising from primary studies to generate second-order concepts and developing a "line or argument."

Meta-narrative mapping The qualitative synthesis method of abstracting ideas to provide comprehensive explanations of historical experiences or knowledge.

Meta-study The qualitative synthesis method of extending knowledge beyond the thematic presentation of primary studies and creating new knowledge derived from this process.

Meta-summary The qualitative synthesis method of aggregating findings from many studies on a specific topic.

Meta-synthesis The qualitative synthesis method that attempts to integrate results from a number of different but interrelated qualitative studies.

Method A series of steps taken to acquire knowledge in qualitative studies.

Mixed methods Using both qualitative and quantitative research design elements to answer research questions.

Narrative review An interpretive process to summarize literature, which often has no explicit methods for searching literature or reporting results.

Naturalism The understanding of behaviors in everyday context.

Negative case This involves searching for and discussing elements of the data that do not support or appear to contradict patterns or explanations that are emerging from data analysis.

Nonprobability sampling (see also purposive and convenience sample) Some people have a greater, but unknown, chance to be included in the sample.

Observation Involves the systematic and detailed observation of events, behaviors, or dialogue for understanding how people live, how they visualize the world, and how they make sense of their experiences (most commonly used in ethnography).

Paradigm An underlying theoretical way of viewing the world.

Participatory research A self-conscious way of empowering people to take effective action toward improving conditions in their lives.

Peer debriefing Formal and informal discussions with peers about the findings.

Persistent observation Extent to which investigation was purposive and assertive.

Phenomenology A qualitative method that describes the lived experiences for several individuals about a concept or the phenomenon. Researchers search for the essence or the central underlying meaning of the experience. From the individual descriptions, general or universal meanings are derived.

Prolonged engagement Intensive involvement with participants and in-depth knowledge of culture. Also includes the length of time in the field.

Post-positivism Phenomena are reflective of a distinct reality that is independent of the observer.

Purposive sampling Choosing specific individuals, groups, or societies based on certain characteristics determined by the intention of the study.

Qualitative study Includes a set of interpretive procedures to understand the meaning of particular activities, experiences, or beliefs in the context of the culture being considered.

Qualitative synthesis The use of interpretive methods to combine study results of studies addressing the same question within a similar epistemological and ontological framework.

Quality guidelines (see quality appraisal) Sets of questions on the different stages of qualitative research planning and designing, conducting the research, analysis, and presentation.

Realist synthesis The qualitative synthesis method of unpacking the mechanism of how complex programs work (or why they fail) in particular contexts and settings.

Reciprocity Shared gains between researchers and participants in terms of equal access to the process and benefits of research. Participants are included as partners in the research process.

Reference management Computer software or programs that hold, index, and maintain all citations, abstracts, and information about articles selected through search strategies.

Referential adequacy Evidence of data collection, such as audiotapes, transcripts, and documents, that connects themes to raw data.

Reflexive journal Diary is kept on a regular basis with entries that reflect ongoing conceptualization of process of research and findings.

Reflexivity Perspective of the researcher is articulated and made transparent throughout the research process.

Refutational synthesis Providing a review of data that explores and explains any contradictions between studies.

Relativism The philosophical assumption that scientific "reality" may look different from different perspectives.

Review of literature An exploration of materials published on a specific topic.

Sampling in qualitative research Qualitative samples tend to be purposive rather than random.

Saturation In a research context, saturation occurs when no new information is uncovered in a study.

Scoping review A review of the literature to determine the depth and breadth of a subject area. Used to find which important areas of inquiry should be prioritized.

Screening A process of going through a large number of studies and selecting those with a specific feature or issue to be included in a study (see also inclusion criteria).

Search filters Pretested strategies to identify and eliminate unrelated studies or lower quality studies from the literature being searched.

Search Strategy A process of information-retrieval that uses specific sources to systematically examine all relevant literature available on a specific topic, population, or social phenomenon.

Search terms The words, truncated values, and search method used in search strategies.

Secondary data Information collected by someone other than the owner of that information. Common secondary data include censuses, surveys, or organizational research.

Sensitizing concepts Ideas, notions, and questions that guide observations and data collection in qualitative research.

Study population The individuals selected to participate in a study.

Subtle realism The philosophical assumption that known reality is only connected to ones' own perspective of that reality.

Systematic review A review of the evidence of a clearly formulated question using explicit methods to identify, select, and critically appraise relevant primary research.

Thematic framework A web of interrelated concepts to guide research and the measurement and statistical tools to be used.

Theoretical sampling Purposeful selection of individuals to include because of the intended purposes of study.

Theoretical validity Deals with the constructions that researchers create and apply in their research and whether these theories and ways of describing are valid. Asks if we are measuring what we think we are measuring.

Transferability The ability to accurately pass the results of one study to another individual, group, or setting accurately.

Transparency Includes the openness, communication, and accountability of research.

Triangulation Refers to the use of two or more methods to purposefully double-checking (or more) the results.

Trustworthiness criteria The state and quality of research or specific elements in research that are reliable and accurate in their measurement of specific phenomenon.

Unpublished papers Academic papers that for one reason or another have not been published in an academic journal. They may be used on Web sites, in government documents, and for other purposes that may not be academic in nature.

References

Abell, P. (1990). *Methodological achievements in sociology over the past few decades with special reference to the interplay of qualitative and quantitative methods.* London: Macmillan.

American Human Association (2005). Strategies to respond to the research needs of family group Conferencing. *FGDM Issues in Brief.* Retrieved from http://www.americanhumane.org/assets/pdfs/children/pc-fgdm-ib-strategies-research-needs.pdf

Anastas, J. W. (2004). Quality in qualitative evaluation: Issues and possible answers. *Research on Social Work Practice, 14*(1), 57–65.

Anfara, V. A., Jr., Brown, K. M., & Mangione, T. L. (2002). Qualitative analysis on stage: Making the research process more public. *Educational Researcher, 31*(7), 28–38.

Angen, M. J. (2000). Evaluating interpretive inquiry: Reviewing the validity debate and opening the dialogue. *Qualitative Health Research, 10*(3), 378–395.

Arksey, H., & O'Malley, L. (2005). Scoping studies: Towards a methodological framework. *International Journal of Social Research Methodology, 8*(1), 19–32.

Attree P. (2004). Growing up in disadvantage: A systematic review of the qualitative evidence. *Child: Care, Health & Development, 30*(6), 679–689.

Attree, P. (2005). Parenting support in the context of poverty: A meta-synthesis of the qualitative evidence. *Health & Social Care in the Community, 13*(4), 330–337.

Atkins, D. (2007). Creating and synthesizing evidence with decision makers in mind: Integrating evidence from clinical trials and other study designs. *Medical Care, 45*, S16–5S22.

Bailey, P. H. (1996). Assuring quality in narrative analysis. *Western Journal of Nursing Research, 18*(2), 186–194.

Banner, D. J., & Albarrran, J. W. (2009). Computer-assisted qualitative data analysis software: A review. *Canadian Journal of Cardiovascular Nursing, 19*(3), 24–31.

Barbour, R. S. (1998). Mixing qualitative methods: Quality assurance or qualitative quagmire? *Quality Health Research, 8,* 352–361.

Barbour, R. S. (2003). The newfound credibility of qualitative research? Tales of technical essentialism and co-option. *Qualitative Health Research, 13*(7), 1019–1027.

Barrera, F. (2006). Impact of private provision of public education: Empirical evidence from Bogotá's concession schools. World Bank Policy Research Working Paper 4121. Retrieved from http://www-wds.worldbank.org/external/default/ WDSContentServer/IW3P/IB/2007/01/26/000016406_20070126111542/ Rendered/INDEX/wps4121.txt.

Barroso, J., Gallup, C. J., Sandelowski, M., Meynell, J., Pearce, P. F., & Collins, L. J. (2003). The challenge of searching for and retrieving qualitative studies. *Western Journal of Nursing Research, 25,* 153–178.

Barroso, J., & Powell-Cope, G. M. (2000). Metasynthesis of qualitative research on living with HIV infection. *Qualitative Health Research, 10*(3), 340–353.

Barroso, J., Sandelowski, M., & Voils, C. I. (2006). Research results have expiration dates: Ensuring timely systematic reviews. *Journal of Evaluation in Clinical Practice, 12,* 454–462.

Baskerville, R., & Wood-Harper, A. (1996). A critical perspective on action research as a method for information systems research. *Journal of Information Technology, 11,* 235–246.

Bate, S. P., & Robert, G. (2002). Knowledge management and communities of practice in the private sector: Lessons for modernizing the national health service in England and Wales. *Public Administration, 80,* 643–663.

Beck, C. (2003). Seeing the forest for the trees: A qualitative synthesis project. *Journal of Nursing Education, 42,* 318–323.

Bell, M. (1996). An account of the experiences of 51 families involved in an initial child protection conference. *Child and Family Social Work, 1,* 43–55.

Bell, M. (1999). Working in partnership in child protection: The conflicts. *British Journal of Social Work, 29*(3), 437–455.

Bell, M., & Wilson, K. (2006). Children's views of family group conferences. *British Journal of Social Work, 36*(4), 671–681.

Berger, P. L., & Luckmann, T., (1966). *The social construction of reality.* Garden City, NY: Anchor.

Bertero, C., & Chamberlain Wilmoth, M. (2007). Breast cancer diagnosis and its treatment affecting the self: A meta-synthesis. *Cancer Nursing, 30*(3), 194–202.

Black, N. (1994). Why we need qualitative research. *Journal of Epidemiology and Community Health, 48,* 425–426.

Bondas, T., & Hall, E. O. C. (2007). Challenges in approaching meta-synthesis research. *Qualitative Health Research, 17*(1), 113–121.

Booth, A. (1996). In search of the evidence: Informing effective practice. *Journal of Clinical Effectiveness, 1*(1), 25–29.

Booth, A. (2001). *Cochrane of cock-eyed? How should we conduct systematic reviews of qualitative research?* Paper presented at the Qualitative Evidence-Based Practice Conference: Taking a critical stance, Coventry University.

Booth, A. (2006). "Brimful of STARLITE": Toward standards for reporting literature searches. *Journal of the Medical Library Association, 94,* 421–429.

Boulton, M., & Fitzpatrick, R. (1994). Quality in qualitative research. *Critical Public Health, 5*(3), 19–26.

Britten, N., Campbell, R., Pope C., Donovan, J., Morgan, M., & Pill, R. (2002). Using meta ethnography to synthesise qualitative research: A worked example. *Journal of Health Services Research & Policy, 7,* 209–215.

Brodie, K. A. (2008). *Family group conference: An exploratory study describing the relationship between an internal agency environment and the process* (doctoral dissertation). Howard University, Washington, D.C.

Brown, L. (2007). The adoption and implementation of a service innovation in a social work setting—A case study of family group conferencing in the UK. *Social Policy and Society, 6*(3), 321–332.

Buchanan, A., & Ritchie, C. (2004). *What works for troubled children* (rev. ed.). London: Barnardo's/Russell Press.

Campbell Collaboration (2001) Guidelines for preparation of review protocols. Retrieved from www.campbellcollaboration.org

Campbell Collaboration Library. Retrieved from http://www.campbell-collaboration.org/library.php.

Campbell, R., Pound, P., Pope, C., Britten, N., Pill, R., Morgan, M., & Donovan, J. (2003). Evaluating metaethnography: A synthesis of qualitative research on lay experiences of diabetes and diabetes care. *Social Science & Medicine, 56*(4), 671–684.

Carnevale, F. A. (2002). Authentic qualitative research and the quest for method-ological rigour. *Canadian Journal of Nursing Research, 34*(2), 121–128.

Cashmore, J. (2000). What the research tells us: Permanency planning, adoption and foster care. *Children Australia, 25,* 17–22.

Chan, A., Hróbjartsson, A., Haahr, M., Gøtzsche, P., & Altman, D. (2004). Empirical evidence for selective reporting of outcomes in random-ized trials: Comparison of protocols to published articles. *JAMA, 291*(20), 2457–2465.

Charmaz, K. (1983). The grounded theory method: An explication and interpre-tation. In Robert M. Emerson (Ed.), *Contemporary field Research: A Collection of Readings* (pp. 109–128). Boston: Little, Brown and Company.

Charmaz, K. (2000). Grounded theory: Objectivist and constructivist methods. In N. Denzin & Y. Lincoln (Eds.), *Handbook of qualitative research* (2d ed., pp. 509–536). Thousand Oaks, CA: Sage.

Charmaz, K. (2004). Premises, principles, and practices in qualitative research: Revisiting the foundations. *Qualitative Health Research, 14*(7), 976–993.

Coffey, A., & Atkinson, P. (1996). *Making sense of qualitative data: Complementary research strategies.* London: Sage.

Coffey, A., Holbrook, B., & Atkinson, P. (1996). Qualitative data analysis: Technologies and representations. *Sociological Research Online, 1*(1). DOI:10.4135/9780857028211. Retrieved from http://www.socresonline.org. uk/1/1/4.html.

Connolly, M. (1994). An act of empowerment: The Children, Young Persons and Their Families Act (1989). *British Journal of Social Work, 24*(1), 87–100.

Connolly, M. (2004). *Fifteen years of family group conferencing: Coordinators talk about their experiences in Aotearoa, New Zealand.* Unpublished research report. University of Canterbury, Christchurch, NZ.

Connolly, M. (2006). Fifteen years of family group conferencing: Coordinators talk about their experiences in Aotearoa New Zealand. *British Journal of Social Work, 36,* 523–540.

Cooper, H. (1998). *Synthesizing research: A guide for literature reviews* (3rd ed.). Thousand Oaks: CA: Sage.

Cooper, H., & Hedges, L. (Eds.). (1994). *The handbook of research synthesis.* New York: Russell Sage Foundation.

Corden, A., & Sainsbury, R. (2006). *Using verbatim quotations in reporting qualitative social research: Researchers' views.* Social Policy Research Unit, University of York. Retrieved from http://www.york.ac.uk/inst/spru/pubs/ pdf/verbquotresearch.pdf.

Crea, T., & Berzin, S. (2008). Family involved in child welfare decision-making: Strategies and research on inclusive practices. *Journal of Public Child Welfare, 3*(3), 305–327.

Creswell, J. W. (1998). *Qualitative inquiry and research design: Choosing among five traditions.* Thousand Oaks, CA: Sage.

Creswell, J. W. (2002). *Educational research: Planning, conducting, and evaluating quantitative and qualitative research.* Upper Saddle River, NJ: Pearson Education.

Creswell, J. W. (2003). *Research design: Qualitative, quantitative, and mixed methods approaches* (2nd ed.). Thousand Oaks, CA: Sage.

Creswell, J. W. (2006). *Qualitative inquiry and research design: Choosing among five traditions.* Thousand Oaks, CA: Sage.

Creswell, J. W. (2007). *Qualitative inquiry and research design. Choosing among five approaches* (2nd ed.). Thousand Oaks, CA: Sage.

Creswell, J. W. (2009). *Research design: Qualitative, quantitative, and mixed methods approaches* (3rd ed.). Los Angles: Sage.

Creswell, J. W., & Maietta, R. C. (2002). Qualitative data analysis software. In D. C. Miller & N. J. Salkind (Eds.), *Handbook of research design and social measurement* (6th ed., pp. 143–200). Thousand Oaks, CA: Sage Publications.

Creswell, J. W., & Miller, D. L. (2000). Determining validity in qualitative inquiry. *Theory into Practice, 39*(3), 124–131.

Cunning S, & Bartlett D. (2006). Family group conferencing: Assessing the long-term effectiveness of an alternative approach in child protection. Final report. Centre of Excellence for Child Welfare Website. Retrieved from http://www.cecw-cepb.ca/files/file/en/Final%20Report%20Family%20Grp%20Conferencing%20March2007.pdf.

Cutcliffe, J. R., & McKenna, H. P. (1999). Establishing the credibility of qualitative research findings: The plot thickens. *Journal of Advanced Nursing, 30*(2), 374–380.

Davies, P. (2003). What do we know already? In Cabinet Office (Ed.), *The magenta book: Guidance notes for policy evaluation and analysis.* London: Government Chief Social Researcher's Office, Cabinet Office.

Davis, L. H. (1994). Relating work to adult higher education. *Journal of Continuing Higher Education, 42*(1), 17–22.

Dawson, A., & Yancey, B. (2006). *Youth participants speak about their family group conference.* Washington, D.C.: American Humane Association. Retrieved from http://www.americanhumane.org/assets/pdfs/children/fgdm/pc-fgdm-ib-youth-participants.pdf.

Denscombe, M. (2008). Communities of practice: A research paradigm for the mixed methods approach. *Journal of Mixed Methods Research, 2*(3), 270–283.

Denyer, D., & D. Tranfield. (2006). Using qualitative research synthesis to build an actionable knowledge base. *Management Decision, 44*(2), 213.

Denzin, N. K. (1978). *The research act: A theoretical introduction to sociological methods.* New York: McGraw-Hill.

Denzin, N. K., & Lincoln, Y. S. (Eds.). (1994). *Handbook of qualitative research.* Thousand Oaks, CA: Sage.

Denzin, N. K., & Lincoln, Y. S. (Eds.). (2000). *Handbook of qualitative research* (2nd ed.). Thousand Oaks, CA: Sage.

Dixon-Woods, M., Agarwal, S., Jones, D., Young, B., & Sutton, A. (2005). Synthesising qualitative and quantitative evidence: A review of possible methods. *Journal of Health Services & Research Policy, 10*(1), 45–53.

Dixon-Woods, M., Agarwal, S., Young, B., Jones, D., & Sutton, A. (2004). *Integrative approaches to qualitative and quantitative evidence.* London: Health Development Agency.

Dixon-Woods, M., Bonas, S., Booth, A., Jones, D. R., Miller, T., Sutton, A. J., . . . Young, B. (2006). How can systematic reviews incorporate qualitative research? A critical perspective. *Qualitative Research, 6*, 27–44.

Dixon-Woods, M., Cavers, D., Agarwal, S., Annandale, E., Arthur, A., Harvey, J., . . . Sutton, A. J. (2006). Conducting a critical interpretive review of the literature on access to healthcare by vulnerable groups. *BMC Medical Research Methodology, 6*(35). Retrieved from http://www.biomedcentral.com/content/pdf/1471-2288-6-35.pdf doi:10.1186/1471-2288-6-35.

Dixon-Woods, M., & Fitzpatrick, R. (2001). Qualitative research in systematic reviews. *BMJ, 323*, 65–66.

Dixon-Woods, M., Fitzpatrick, R., & Roberts, K. (2001). Including qualitative research in systematic reviews: Opportunities and problems. *Journal of Evaluation in Clinical Practice, 7*(2), 125–133.

Dixon-Woods, M., Shaw, R. L., Agarwal, S., & Smith, J. A. (2004). The problem of appraising qualitative research. *Quality & Safety in Healthcare, 13*(3), 223–225.

Doyle, L. H. (2003). Synthesis through meta-ethnography: Paradoxes, enhancements, and possibilities. *Qualitative Research, 3*(3), 321–344.

Draucker, C. B., Martsolf, D. S., Ross., R., Cook, C. B., Stidham, A. W., & Mweemba, P. (2009). The essence of healing from sexual violence: A qualitative metasynthesis. *Research in Nursing and Health, 32*, 366–378.

Drisko, J. (1997). Strengthening qualitative studies and reports: Standards to enhance academic integrity. *Journal of Social Work Education, 33*, 1–13.

Drisko, J. (1998). Using qualitative data analysis software. *Journal of Technology in Human Services, 15*(1), 1–19.

Drisko, J. W. (2004). Qualitative data analysis software: A user's appraisal. In D. Padgett (Ed.), *The qualitative research experience* (rev. ed., pp. 193–209). Belmont, CA: Wadsworth.

Eaves, Y. (2001). A synthesis technique for grounded theory data analysis. *Journal of Advanced Nursing, 35*(5), 654–663.

Egger, M., Davey-Smith, G., Schneider, M., & Minder, C. (1997). Bias in meta-analysis detected by a simple, graphical test. *BMJ, 315*, 629–634.

Egger, M., Smith, D., & Phillips, A. (1997). Meta-analysis principles and procedures. *BMJ, 315*, 1533–1537.

Erlandson, D., Harris, E., Skipper, B., & Allen., S. (1993). *Doing naturalistic inquiry: A guide to methods.* London: Sage Publications.

Espíndola, C. R., & Blay, S. C. (2009). Anorexia nervosa's meaning to patients: A qualitative synthesis. *Psychopathology, 42*, 64–80.

Evans, D. (2002). Database searches for qualitative research. *Journal of the Medical Library Association, 90*, 290–293.

Evans, D., & FitzGerald, M. (2002). Reasons for physically restraining patients and residents: A systematic review and content analysis. *International Journal of Nursing Studies, 39,* 735–743.

Fetterman, D. (1988). Qualitative approaches to evaluating education. *Educational Research, 17*(8), 17–23.

Finfgeld, D. (1999). Courage as a process of pushing beyond the struggle. *Qualitative Health Research, 9,* 803–814.

Finfgeld, D. L. (2003). Metasynthesis: The state of the art—so far. *Qualitative Health Research, 13*(7), 893–904.

Finfgeld-Connett, D. (2009). Management of aggression among demented or brain-injured patients. *Clinical Nursing Research, 18*(3), 272–287.

Finfgeld-Connett, D. (2010). Generalizability and transferability of meta-synthesis research findings. *Journal of Advanced Nursing, 66*(2), 246–254.

Finlay, L. (2002). "Outing" the researcher: The provenance, process, and practice of reflexivity. *Qualitative Health Research, 12*(4), 531–545.

Flemming, K. (2007). Research methodologies. Synthesis of qualitative research and evidenced-based nursing. *British Journal of Nursing, 16,* 616–620.

Flemming, K., & Briggs, M. (2007). Electronic searching to locate qualitative research: Evaluation of three strategies. *Journal of Advanced Nursing, 57*(1), 95–100.

Forchuk, C., & Roberts, J. (1993). How to critique qualitative health research articles. *Canadian Journal of Nursing Research, 25*(4), 47–56.

Frankel, R. M. (1999). Standards of qualitative research. In B. F. Crabtree & W. L. Miller (Eds.), *Doing qualitative research* (2nd ed., pp. 333–346). Thousand Oaks, CA: Sage.

Gallagher, F., & Jasper, M. (2003). Health visitors' experiences of family group conferences in relation to child protection planning: A phenomenological study. *Journal of Nursing Management, 11*(6), 377–386.

Gearing, R., Saini, M., & McNeill, T. (2007). Experiences and implications of social workers practicing in a pediatric hospital environment affected by SARS. *Health and Social Work, 31*(1), 17–27.

Gibbs, L. E. (2003). Evidence-based practice for the helping professions: A practical guide with integrated multimedia. Pacific Grove, CA: Brooks /Cole.

Gilgun, J. (2009). The four consensus of qualitative research. *Qualitative Health Research, 19*(6), 868–874.

Glaser, B. G. (1978). *Theoretical sensitivity.* Mill Valley, CA: Sociology Press.

Glaser, B. G., & Strauss, A. (1967). *The discovery of grounded theory.* Chicago: Aldine.

Glaser, B. G., & Strauss, A. (1971). *Status passage.* Chicago: Aldine.

Glasziou, P., Irwin, L., Bain, C., & Colditz, G. (2001). *Systematic reviews in health care: A practical guide.* Melbourne: Cambridge University Press.

Glisson, C. (1990). *A systematic assessment of the social work literature: Trends in social work research.* Knoxville: University of Tennessee, College of Social Work.

Golafshani, N. (2003). Understanding reliability and validity in qualitative research. *The Qualitative Report, 8*(4), 597–606.

Goldstein, J. R. (2006). How late can first births be postponed? Some illustrative population level calculations. *Vienna Yearbook of Population Research, 4,* 153–165.

Gollop, R., Ketley, D., Buchanan, D., Whitby, E., Lamont, S., Jones, J., . . . & Fitzgerald, L. (2006). "Research into practice": A model for healthcare management research? *Evidence & Policy: A Journal of Research, Debate and Practice, 2*(2), 257–267.

Gough, D., & Elbourne, D. (2002). Systematic research synthesis to inform policy, practice and democratic debate. *Social Policy and Society, 1,* 225–236.

Graham, I. D., Logan, J., Harrison, M. B., Straus, S. E., Tetroe, J., Caswell, W., & Robinson, N. (2006). Lost in knowledge translation: Time for a map? *Journal of Continuing Education in the Health Professions, 26,* 13–24.

Grant, M. J. (2004). How does your searching grow? A survey of search preferences and the use of optimal search strategies in the identification of qualitative research. *Health Information and Libraries Journal, 21*(1), 21–32.

Greene, J. (2008). Is mixed methods social inquiry a distinctive methodology? *Journal of Mixed Methods Research, 2*(1), 7–22.

Greene, J. C. (1994). Qualitative programme evaluation. In N. K. Denzin & Y. S. Lincoln (Eds.), *Handbook of qualitative research* (pp. 530–545). London: Sage Publications.

Greene, J. C. (2007). *Mixed methods in social inquiry.* New York: John Wiley & Sons, Publishers.

Greene, J. C., & Caracelli, V. J. (Eds.). (1997). *Advances in mixed-method evaluation: The challenges and benefits of integrated diverse paradigms.* San Francisco: Jossey-Bass.

Greene, J. C., Caracelli, V. J., & Graham, W. F. (1989). Toward a conceptual framework for mixed-method evaluation designs. *Educational Evaluation and Policy Analysis, 11*(3), 255–274.

Greenhalgh, T., Glenn, R., Macfarlane, F., Bate, P., & Kyriakidou, O. (2004). Diffusion of innovations in service organizations: Systematic review and recommendations. *Milbank Quarterly, 82*(4), 581–629.

Greenhalgh, T., & Taylor, R. (1997). How to read a paper: Papers that go beyond numbers (qualitative research). *BMJ, 315,* 595–616.

Grimshaw, J. M., Thomas, R. E., MacLennan, G., Fraser, C., Ramsay, C., Vale, L. . . . Donaldson, C. (2004). Effectiveness and efficiency of guideline dissemination and implementation strategies. *Health Technology Assessment, 8*(6). Retrieved from http://www.hta.ac.uk/fullmono/mon806.pdf.

Grinnell, R. M. (1997). *Social work research and evaluation: Quantitative and qualitative approaches* (5th ed.). Itasca, IL: F. E. Peacock Publishers, Inc.

Guba, E. G., & Lincoln, Y. S. (1989). *Fourth generation evaluation.* Newbury Park, CA: Sage.

Guba, E. G., & Lincoln, Y. S. (2005). Paradigmatic controversies, contradictions, and emerging confluences. In N. K. Denzin & Y. S. Lincoln (Eds.), *The Sage handbook of qualitative research* (3rd ed., pp. 191–215). Thousand Oaks, CA: Sage.

Guyette, S. (1983). *Community-based research: A handbook for Native Americans.* Los Angeles: University of California American Indian Studies Center.

Hall, B. (1979). Knowledge as a commodity and participatory research. *Prospects, 9*(4), 393–408.

Hammerstrom, K., Wade, A., & Klint Jorgensen, A. M. (2010). *Searching for studies: A guide to information retrieval for Campbell Systematic Reviews.* Campbell Systematic Reviews. Supplement 1. Retrieved from www.campbellcollaboration.org/resources/research/.

Harden, A., Garcia, J., Oliver, S., Rees, R., Shepherd, J., Brunton, G., & Oakley, A. (2004). Applying systematic review methods to studies of people's views: An example from public health research. *Journal of Epidemiology & Community Health, 58*(9), 794–800.

Harden, A., Oakley, A., & Oliver, S. (2001). Peer-delivered health promotion for young people: A systematic review of different study designs. *Health Education Journal, 60,* 339–353.

Harden, A., & Thomas, J. (2005). Methodological issues in combining diverse study types in systematic reviews. *International Journal of Social Research Methodology, 8*(3), 257–271.

Harris, M. M. (1999). Practice network: I-O psychology.com—the internet and I-O psychology. *The Industrial-Organizational Psychologist, 36,* 89–93.

Harrison, M. I. (1994). *Diagnosing organizations. Methods, models, and processes* (2nd ed.). Thousand Oaks, CA: Sage.

Hartley, J., Sydes, M., & Blurton, A. (1996). Obtaining information accurately and quickly: Are structured abstracts more efficient? *Journal of Information Science, 22*(5), 349–356.

Harvey, D. (2007). Understanding Australian rural women's ways of achieving health and wellbeing: A metasynthesis of the literature. *Rural and Remote Health, 7,* [Online]. Retrieved from http://rrh.deakin.edu.au PubMed: 17935458.

Haynes, R., Sackett, D., Gray, J., Cook, D. J., & Guyatt, G. H. (1996). Transferring evidence from research into practice: 1. The role of clinical care research evidence in clinical decisions. *ACP Journal Club, 125,* A14–16.

Haynes, R. B., Devereaux, P. J., & Guyatt, G. H. (2002). Clinical expertise in the era of evidence-based medicine and patient choice. *ACP Journal Club, 136*(2), A11–A14.

Higgins J. P. T., & Green S. (Eds.). (2006). *Formulating the problem. Cochrane handbook for systematic reviews of interventions 4.2.6 (IV).* Chichester, UK: The Cochrane Collaboration John Wiley & Sons, Ltd.

Higgins, J. P. T., & Green, S (Eds.). (2008). *Cochrane handbook for systematic reviews of interventions version 5.0.1.* Chichester, UK: The Cochrane Collaboration John Wiley & Sons, Ltd.

Holland, S., & O'Neil, S. (2006). We had to be there to make sure it was what we wanted: Enabling children's participation in family decision-making through the Family Group Conference. *Childhood, 13*(1), 91–111.

Holland, S., & Rivett, M. (2008). Everyone started shouting: Making connections between the process of family group conferences and family therapy practice. *British Journal of Social Work, 38,* 21–38.

Holloway, I., & Wheeler, S. (1995). Ethical issues in qualitative nursing research. *Nursing Ethics, 2*(3), 223–232.

Howe, K. R., (1988). Against the quantitative-qualitative incompatibility thesis (or dogmas diehard). *Educational researcher, 17,* 10–16.

Inui, T. S., & Frankel, R. M. (1991). Evaluating the quality of qualitative research: A proposal pro-tem. *Journal of General Internal Medicine, 6*(5), 485–486.

Jack, S. M. (2006). Utility of qualitative research findings in evidence-based public health practice. *Public Health Nursing, 23,* 277–283.

Jensen, L., & Allen, M. (1996). Meta-synthesis of qualitative findings. *Qualitative Health Research, 6,* 553–560.

Jensen, L. A., & Allen, M. N. (1994). A synthesis of qualitative research on wellness-illness. *Qualitative Health Research, 4*(4), 349–369.

Johnson, B., & Christenson, L. (2008). *Educational research: Quantitative, qualitative, and mixed approached* (3rd ed.). Thousand Oaks, CA: Sage.

Johnson, R. B., & Onwuegbuzie, A. J. (2004). Mixed methods research: A research paradigm whose time has come. *Educational Researcher, 33*(7), 14–26.

Kane, G. A., Wood, V. A., & Barlow, J. (2007). Parenting programmes: A systematic review and synthesis of qualitative research Child. *Care, Health, and Development, 33*(6), 784–793.

Kaplan, B., & Duchon, D. (1988). Combining qualitative and quantitative approaches in information systems research: A case study. *Management Information Systems Quarterly, 12*(4), 571–584.

Karim, K. (2001). Assessing the strengths and weaknesses of action research. *Nursing Standard, 15*(26), 33–35.

Khan, K., Kunz, R., Kleijnen, J., & Antle, G. (2003). *Systematic reviews to support evidence-based medicine: How to review and apply findings of healthcare research.* London: Royal Society of Medicine Press.

Kearney, M. (1998). Ready to wear: Discovering grounded formal theory. *Research in Nursing & Health, 21*(2), 179–186.

Kearney, M. H. (2001). Levels and applications of qualitative research evidence. *Research in Nursing and Health, 24,* 145–153.

Kluger, M., Alexander, G., & Curtis, P. (2000). *What works in child welfare.* New York: Child Welfare League of America, Inc.

Lach, L., McNeil, T., & Nicholas, D. (2005). *Quality in qualitative research.* University of Toronto Unpublished document created for teaching purposes.

Larsson, R. (1993). Case survey methodology: Quantitative analysis of patterns across case studies. *Academy of Management Journal, 36*(6), 1515–1546.

Lavigne, J. V., & Faier-Routman, J. (1993). Correlates of psychological adjustment to pediatric physical disorders: A meta-analytic review and comparison with existing models. *Developmental and Behavioral Pediatrics, 14,* 117–123.

Laws, S., & Kirby, P. (2007). *Under the table or at the table? Supporting children and families in family group conferences: A summary of the Daybreak research.* East Sussex, United Kingdom. Brighton & Hove Children's Fund Partnership. Retrieved from http://www.worldwebwise.co.uk/daybreakfgc/docs/UnderthetableorattheTablesummary.pdf.

Lazaraton, A. (2003). Evaluative criteria for qualitative research in applied linguistics: Whose criteria and whose research? *The Modern Language Journal, 87*(1), 1–12.

Leech, N. L., & Onwuegbuzie, A. J. (2009). A typology of mixed methods research designs. *Quality and Quantity: International Journal of Methodology, 43,* 265–275.

Lemmer, B., Grellier, R., & Stevens, J. (1999). Systematic review of non-random and qualitative research literature: Exploring and uncovering an evidence base for health visiting and decision making. *Qualitative Health Research, 9*(3), 315–328.

Léveillé, S., Trocmé, N., Chamberland, C., & Brown, I. (2011). *Partnerships in child welfare research.* Toronto: Centre of Excellence for Child Welfare.

Lewins, A. (2008). CAQDAS: Computer assisted qualitative data analysis. In N. Gielbert (Ed.), *Researching Social Life* (3rd ed., pp. 343–357). London: Sage Publications.

Lewins, A., & Silver, C. (2007). *Using software in qualitative research: A step-by-step guide.* London: Sage Publications.

Lewis, J. (1998), Building an evidence-based approach to social interventions, *Children and Society, 12,* (pp. 136–140).

Lewis, R. B. (2004). NVivo 2.0 and ATLAS.ti 5.0: A comparative review of two popular qualitative data-analysis programs. *Field Methods, 16*(4), 439–464.

Lincoln, Y. (1995). Emerging criteria for quality in qualitative and interpretive research. *Quality Inquiry, 1*(3), 275–289.

Lincoln, Y., & Guba, E. (1985). *Naturalistic inquiry.* Beverley Hills, CA: Sage Publications.

Littell, J. H., & Corcoran, J. (2010). Systematic reviews. In B. Thyer (Ed.), *The handbook of social work research* (2nd ed.). Thousand Oaks, CA: Sage Publications.

Littell, J., Corcoran, J., & Pallai, V. (2008). *Systematic reviews and meta-analysis.* New York: Oxford University Press.

Lloyd, J. M. (2005). Role development and effective practice in specialist and advanced practice roles in acute hospital settings: Systematic review and meta-synthesis. *Journal of Advanced Nursing, 49*(2), 191–209.

Löschper, G. (2000). Crime and social control as fields of qualitative research in the social sciences. *Forum Qualitative Sozialforschung/Forum: Qualitative Social Research, North America, 1*(1) Art. 9. Retrieved from http://nbn-resolving. de/urn:nbn:de:0114-fqs000195.

Lowe, H. J, & Barnett, G. O. (1994). Understanding and using the medical subject headings (MeSH) vocabulary to perform literature searches. *JAMA, 271*(14), 1103–1108.

Madill, A., Jordan, A., & Shirley, C. (2000). Objectivity and reliability in qualitative analysis: Realist, contextualist and radical constructionist epistemologies. *British Journal of Psychology, 91*(1), 1–20.

Maluccio, A., & Daly, J. (2000). Family group conferencing as "good" child welfare practice. In G. Burford & J. Hudson (Eds.), *Family group conferencing. New directions in community-centered child and family practice* (pp. 65–71). New York: Aldine De Gruyter.

Manten, A. A. (1973). Scientific literature reviews. *Scholarly Publishing, 5,* 75–89.

Martsolf, D. S., Draucker, C. B., Cook, C. B., Ross, R., Warner, A., & Mweemba, P. (2010). A meta-summary of qualitative findings about professional services for survivors of sexual violence. *Qualitative Report, 15*(3), 644–657.

Mason, J. (1996). *Qualitative researching.* London: Sage.

Maykut, P., & Morehouse, R. (1994). *Beginning qualitative research: A philosophical and practical guide.* London: Falmer Press.

Mays, N., & Pope, C. (1995). Qualitative research: Rigour and qualitative research. *BMJ, 311*(6997), 109–112.

Mays N., Pope, C., & Popay, J. (2005). Systematically reviewing qualitative and quantitative evidence to inform management and policy-making in the health field. *Journal of Health Services of Research Policy, 10*(1), 6–20.

McCready, A., & Donnelly, A. (2005). *Family group conference project: Homefirst Community Trust.* Northland Ireland. Retrieved from http://www.fgcforumni. org/cmsfiles/files/fgc-evaluation-report-march-2005-homefirst-trust.

McDermott, E., Graham, H., & Hamilton, V. (2004). *Experience of being a teenage mother in the UK: A report of a systematic review of qualitative studies, The Centre for Evidence-based Public Health Policy*, The Social and Public Health Services Unit, Glasgow: University of Glasgow.

McGaw S. (2000). *What works for parents with learning disabilities?* Barnardos. Retrieved from http://www.barnardos.org.uk/resources/researchpublications/documents/WWPARWLD.PDF.

McInnes, E., & Wimpenny, P. (2008). Using qualitative assessment and review instrument software to synthesise studies on older people's views and experiences of falls prevention. *International Journal of Evidence-based Healthcare, 6*(3), 337–344.

McIntosh, N. (1994). *Structured abstracts and information transfer* (British Library R&D Report 6142). London: British Library.

McKibbon, K. A., & Gadd, C. S. (2006). A quantitative analysis of qualitative studies in clinical journals for the 2000 publishing year. *BMC Medical Inform Decision Making.* Retrieved from http://www.biomedcentral.com/1472–6947/4/11.

McKibbon, K. A., Wilczynski, N. L., & Haynes, R. B. (2006). Developing optimal search strategies for retrieving qualitative studies in PsycINFO. *Evaluation & the Health Professions, 29*(4), 440–454.

Meadows-Oliver, M. (2006). Homeless adolescent mothers: A metasynthesis of their life experiences. *Journal of Pediatric Nursing, 21,* 340–349.

Meeker, M. A., & Jezewski, M. A. (2008). Metasynthesis: Withdrawing life-sustaining treatments: The experience of family decision-makers. *Journal of Clinical Nursing, 18*(2), 163–173.

Merriam, S. B. (1988). *Case study research in education: A qualitative approach.* San Francisco: Jossey-Bass.

Miles, M. B., & Huberman, M. (1994). *Qualitative data analysis: A sourcebook of new methods* (2d ed.). Beverly Hills, CA: Sage Publications.

Mishler, E. G. (1979). Meaning in context: Is there any other kind? *Harvard Educational Review, 49,* 1–19.

Mishna, F., Cook, C., Saini, M., Wu, M-J., & MacFadden, R., (2011). Prevention and intervention of cyber abuse targeting children and adolescents: A systematic review to evaluate current approaches. *Research on Social Work Practice, 21*(1), 5–14. doi: 10.1177/1049731509351988.

Morgan, D. (1998). Practical strategies for combining qualitative and quantitative methods: Applications to health research. *Qualitative Health Research, 8*(3), 362–376.

Morse, J. (2006). The politics of evidence. *Qualitative Health Research, 16,* 395–404.

Morse, J. M., & Singleton, J. (2001). Exploring the technical aspects of "fit" in qualitative research. *Qualitative Health Research, 11*(6), 841–847.

Moustakas, C. (1994). *Phenomenological research methods.* Thousand Oaks, CA: Sage.

Mulrow, C. (1994). Systematic reviews: Rationale for systematic reviews. *BMJ, 309,* 597–599.

Muncey, T. (2009). An overview of mixed methods research. *Journal of Research in Nursing, 14*(2), 187–188.

Murphy, E., Dingwall, R., Greenbatch, D., Parker, S., & Watson, P. (1998). Qualitative research methods in health technology assessment: A review of the literature. *Health Technology Assessment, 2,* iii–ix, 1–274.

Neff, D. (2006). *Perceptions of procedural justice in child protection: A study of family group conferencing* (doctoral dissertation). Social Welfare, Graduate Division of the University of Hawaii.

Neuman, W. L. (2003). *The meanings of methodology: Social research methods* (5th ed.). Boston, MA: Allyn & Bacon.

Newman, I., & Benz, C. R. (1998). *Qualitative-quantitative research methodology: Exploring the interactive continuum.* Carbondale: Southern Illinois University Press.

Newman, M., Thompson, C., & Roberts, A. P. (2006). Helping practitioners understand the contribution of qualitative research to evidence-based practice. *Evidence Based Nursing, 9,* 4–7.

Nicholas, D., Globerman, J., Antle, B., McNeil, T., & Lach, L. (2006). Processes of meta-study: A study of psychosocial adaptation to childhood chronic health conditions. *International Journal of Qualitative Methods, 5*(1), 1–10. Retrieved from http://www.ualberta.ca/ ijqm/english/engframeset.html.

Noblit, G. W., & Hare, R. D. (1988). *Meta-ethnography: Synthesizing qualitative studies.* Newbury Park, CA: Sage Publications.

Noyes, J., & Popay, J. (2006). Directly observed therapy and tuberculosis: How can a systematic review of qualitative research contribute to improving services? A qualitative meta-synthesis. *Journal of Advanced Nursing, 5*(2), 231–249.

O'Campo, P., Kirst, M., Schaefer-McDaniel, N., Firestone, M., Scott, A., & McShane, K. (2009). Community-based services for homeless adults experiencing concurrent mental health and substance use disorders: A realist approach to synthesizing evidence. *Journal of Urban Health, 86*(6), 965–989.

Onwuegbuzie A.J. & Leech, N.L. (2007a). A call for qualitative power analyses. *Quality & Quantity, 41,* 105–121.

Onwuegbuzie, A. J., & Leech, N. L. (2007b). Sampling designs in qualitative research: Making the sampling process more public. *The Qualitative Report, 12*(2), 238–254.

Onwuegbuzie, A. J., & Leech, N. L. (2007c). Validity and qualitative research: An oxymoron? *Quality and Quantity: International Journal of Methodology, 41,* 233–249.

Padgett, D. (1998). *Qualitative methods in social work research*. Thousand Oaks, CA: Sage.

Padgett, D. (2004). The *qualitative research experience*. Belmont, CA: Brooks/Cole.

Padgett, D. (2008). *Qualitative methods in social work research* (2nd ed.). Thousand Oaks, CA: Sage.

Padgett, D. (2009). Qualitative and mixed methods in social work knowledge development. *Social Work, 52*(2), 101–105.

Palinkas, L. A., Schoenwald, S. K., Hoagwood, K., Landsverk, J., Chorpita, B. F., Weisz, J. R., & the Research Network on Youth Mental Health. (2008). An ethnographic study of implementation of evidence-based practice in child mental health: First steps. *Psychiatric Services, 59*, 738–746.

Park, P., Brydon-Miller, M., Hall, B., & Jackson, T. (1993). *Voices of change: Participatory research in the United States and Canada*. Westport, CT: Bergin & Garvey.

Parker, I. (2004). Criteria for qualitative research in psychology. *Qualitative Research in Psychology, 1*(2), 95–106.

Parkinson, P., & Cashmore, J. (2007). Judicial conversations with children in parenting disputes: The views of Australian judges. *International Journal of Law, Policy and the Family, 21*, 160–189.

Parse, R. R. (2007). Building a research culture. *Nursing Science Quarterly, 20*(197), 148–154.

Paterson, B. L., Thorne, S., & Dewis, M. (1998). Adapting to and managing diabetes. *Journal of Nursing School, 30*(1), 57–62.

Paterson, B., Thorne, S. E., Canam, C., & Jillings C. (2001). *Meta-study of qualitative health research: A practical guide to meta-analysis and meta-synthesis*. Thousand Oaks, CA: Sage.

Patton, M. (1990). *Qualitative evaluation and research methods*. Newbury Park, CA: Sage.

Patton, M. Q. (1999). Enhancing the quality and credibility of qualitative analysis. *Health Services Research, 34*(5), 1189–1209.

Patton, M. (2001). *Qualitative evaluation and research methods* (3rd ed.). Thousand Oaks, CA: Sage.

Pawson, R. (2006). *Evidence based policy: A realist perspective*. Thousand Oaks, CA: Sage.

Pawson, R., & Boaz, A. (2004). *Evidence-based policy, theory-based synthesis, user-led review* (ESRC Research Methods Programme Project). Retrieved from www.evidencenetwork.org/project3.asp.

Pawson, R., Greenhalgh, T., Harvey, G., & Walshe, K. (2004). *Realist synthesis: An introduction* (ESRC Research Methods Programme), University of Manchester. Retrieved from http://www.ccsr.ac.uk/methods/publications/documents/RMPmethods2.pdf.

Pawson, R., & Tilley, N. (1997). *Realistic evaluation*. London: Sage.

Pearson, A., Wiechula, R., Court, A., & Lockwood, C. (2005). The JBI model of evidence-based healthcare. *Journal of British I Reports, 3*, 207–216.

Peck, E., & Secker, J. (1999). Quality criteria for qualitative research: Does context make a difference? *Qualitative Health Research, 9*(4), 552–558.

Peek Corbin-Staton, A. (2009). *Contexts of parental involvement: An interpretive synthesis of qualitative literature using the meta-interpretation method* (doctoral dissertation). George Washington University, Washington, D.C.

Petticrew, M., & Roberts, H. (2006). *Systematic reviews in the social sciences: A practical guide*. Oxford: Blackwell.

Phillips, D. C. (2000). *The expanded social scientist's bestiary*. Lanham, MD: Rowman & Littlefield.

Popay, J. (2006). *Incorporating qualitative information in systematic reviews*. Paper presented at the 14th Cochrane Colloquium, Dublin, Ireland.

Popay, J., Arai, L., & Roen, K. (2003). *Exploring methodological and practical issues in the systematic review of factors affecting the implementation of child injury prevention initiatives*. London: Health Development Agency.

Popay, J., Rogers, A., & Williams, G. (1998). Rationale and standards for the systematic review of qualitative literature in health services research. *Qualitative Health Research, 8*(3), 341–351.

Pope, C., & Mays, N. (1995). Qualitative research: Reaching the parts other methods cannot reach: An introduction to qualitative methods in health and health services research. *BMJ, 311*, 42–45.

Pope, C., & Mays, N. (2009). Critical reflections on the rise of qualitative research. *BMJ, 339*, 3425–3425.

Pope, C., Mays, N., & Popay, J. (2007). *Synthesizing qualitative and quantitative health research: A guide to methods*. Berkshire, U.K.: Open University Press.

Pound, P., Britten, N., Morgan, M., Yardley, L., Pope, C., Daker-White, G., & Campbell, R. (2005). Resisting medicines: A synthesis of qualitative studies of medicine taking. *Social Science and Medicine, 61*, 133–155.

Power, R. (2001). Checklists for improving rigour in qualitative research. Never mind the tail (checklist), check out the dog (research). *BMJ, 323*(7311), 514–515.

Quinlan, E., & Quinlan. A., (2010). Representations of rape: Transcending methodological divides. *Journal of Mixed Methods Research, 4*(2), 127–143.

Reid, A., & Gough, S. (2000). Guidelines for reporting and evaluating qualitative research: What are the alternatives? *Environmental Education Research, 6*(1), 59–90.

Reinharz, S. T. (1979). *On becoming a social scientist: From survey research and participant observation to experiential analysis*. San Francisco: Jossey-Bass.

Riessman, C. (1993). *Narrative analysis (qualitative research methods)*. Thousand Oaks, CA: Sage.

Roberts, K., Dixon-Woods, M., Fitzpatrick, R., Abrams, K., & Jones, D. R. (2002). Factors affecting uptake of childhood immunization: A Bayesian synthesis of qualitative and quantitative evidence. *Lancet, 360,* 1596–1599.

Rodwell, M. K. (1987). Naturalistic inquiry: An alternative model for social work assessment. *Social Service Review, 61,* 231–246.

Rossman, G. B., & Wilson, B. L. (1985). Numbers and words: Combining qualitative and quantitative methods in a single large scale evaluation. *Evaluation Review, 9*(5), 627–643.

Royse, D., Thyer, B., Padgett, D., & Logon, T. (2006). *Program evaluation* (4th ed). Belmont, CA: Thomson.

Rubin, A. (2000). Standards for rigor in qualitative inquiry. *Research on Social Work Practice, 10*(2), 173–179.

Ryan, R., Hill, S., Lowe, D., Allen, K., Taylor, M., & Mead, C. (2011). Notification and support for people exposed to the risk of Creutzfeldt-Jakob disease (CJD) (or other prion diseases) through medical treatment (iatrogenically). *Cochrane Database of Systematic Reviews*(3). Art. No.: CD007578. DOI: 10.1002/14651858. CD007578.pub2.

Sackett, D. L., Richardson, W. S., Rosenberg, W., & Haynes, R. B. (1997). *Evidence based medicine. How to practice and teach EBM.* Edinburgh: Churchill Livingstone.

Saini (2011). Qualitative research quality checklist. University of Toronto, Toronto, ON: Unpublished manuscript.

Saini, M., & Birnbaum, R. (2005). Linking judicial decision-making in joint custody awards with evidence–based practice: It is possible? *Canadian Family Law Quarterly, 24,* 139–165.

Saini, M., & Léveillé, S. (2011). Researcher–community partnerships: A systematic synthesis of qualitative research. In S. Léveillé, N. Trocmé, C. Chamberland, & I. Brown (Eds.), *Partnerships in child welfare research.* (pp. 1–42). Toronto: Centre of Excellence for Child Welfare.

Sandelowski M. (1994). Focus on qualitative methods. The use of quotes in qualitative research. *Research in Nursing & Health, 17,* 479–482.

Sandelowski, M. (1995). Focus on qualitative methods: Sample sizes in qualitative research. *Research in Nursing & Health, 18,* 179–183.

Sandelowski, M. (2001). Real qualitative researchers do not count: The use of numbers in qualitative research. *Research in Nursing & Health, 24*(3), 230–240.

Sandelowski, M. (2007). Words that should be seen but not written. *Research in Nursing & Health, 30,* 129–130.

Sandelowski, M., & Barroso, J. (2002). Reading qualitative studies. *International Journal of Qualitative Methods, 1*(1), Article 5. Retrieved from http://www.ualberta.ca/~ijqm/

Sandelowski, M., & Barroso, J. (2003a). Creating metasummaries of qualitative findings. *Nursing Research, 5*, 226–233.

Sandelowski, M., & Barroso, J. (2003b). Toward a metasynthesis of qualitative findings on motherhood in HIV-positive women. *Research in Nursing & Health, 26*, 153–170.

Sandelowski, M., & Barroso, J. (2007). *Handbook for synthesizing qualitative research.* New York: Springer.

Sandelowski, M., Barroso, J., & Voils, C. I. (2007). Using qualitative meta-summary to synthesize qualitative and quantitative descriptive findings. *Research in Nursing & Health, 30*, 99–111.

Sandelowski, M., Docherty, S., & Emden, C. (1997). Focus on qualitative methods, qualitative metasynthesis: Issues and techniques. *Research in Nursing & Health, 20*, 365–371.

Sandelowski, M., Voils, C. I., & Barroso, J. (2006). Defining and designing mixed methods research synthesis studies. *Research in the Schools, 13*(1), 29–40.

Sayer, A. (1992). *Method in social science: A realist approach* (2nd ed.). London: Routledge.

Schreiber, R., Crooks, D., & Stern, P. (1997). Qualitative meta-analysis. In J. Morse (Ed.), *Completing a qualitative project: Details and dialogue.* Thousand Oaks, CA: Sage.

Seidel, J. (1991). Method and madness in the application of computer technology to qualitative data analysis. In N. Fielding & R. M. Lee (Eds.), *Using computers in qualitative research* (pp. 107–116). London: Sage.

Shank, G. (2002). *Qualitative research. A personal skills approach.* Upper Saddle River, NJ: Merrill Prentice Hall.

Shaw, I., & Gould, N. (2001). *Qualitative social work research.* London: Sage.

Shaw, R. L., Booth, A., Sutton, A. J., Miller, T., Smith, J. A., Young, B., . . . Dixon-Woods, M. (2003). Electronic literature searching for systematic review of qualitative literature. *Journal of Epidemiology and Community Health, 57*(1), A15.

Shaw, R. L., Booth, A., Sutton, A. J., Miller, T., Smith, J. A., Young, B., . . . Dixon-Woods, M. (2004). Finding qualitative research: An evaluation of search strategies. *BMC Medical Research Methodology, 4*, 1–5.

Shenton, A. K. (2004). Strategies for ensuring trustworthiness in qualitative research projects. *Education for Information, 22*(2), 63–75.

Sherman, E., & Reid, W. J. (1994). *Qualitative research in social work.* New York: Columbia University Press.

Sherwood, G. (1999). Meta-synthesis: Merging qualitative studies to develop nursing knowledge. *International Journal for Human Caring, 3*, 32–42.

Shlonsky, A., Schumaker, K., Cook, C., Crampton, D., Saini, M., Backe-Hansen, E. & Kowalski, K. (2008). Family Group Decision Makin for children at risk of abuse and neglect (protocol). *Cochrane Database of Systematic*

Reviews, DOI: 10.1002/14651858. CD007984 Retrieved from http://www. campbellcollaboration.org/.

Sibthorpe, B., Bailie, R., Brady, M., Ball, S., Sumner-Dodd, P., & Hall, W. (2002). The demise of a planned randomised controlled trial in an urban Indigenous medical service. *Medical Journal of Australia, 176*, 273–276.

Silver, C., & Fielding, N. (2008). Using computer assisted qualitative data analysis. In C. Willing & W. Stainton-Rogers (Eds.), *The Sage handbook of qualitative research in psychology* (pp. 334–351). London: Sage Publications.

Sinclair, I. (2000). Methods and measurement in evaluative social work. In A. Mullender (Ed.), *Theorising Social Work Research* (Report to ESRC), University of Warwick. Retrieved from http://www.scie.org.uk/publications/misc/tswr/seminar6/sinclair.as.

Slater, L. (2008). Qualitative filters. University of Alberta. Retrieved from http://www.ualberta.ca/~lslater/QualFilters.html.

Smaling, A. (2003). Inductive, analogical, and communicative generalization. *International Journal of Qualitative Methods, 2*, 1, 52–67. Retrieved from http://www.ualberta.ca/~iiqm/backissues/2_1/html/smaling.html.

Smith, J. (1995). Semi structured interviewing and qualitative analysis. In J. A. Smith, R. Harre, & L. V. Langgenhove (Eds.), *Rethinking methods in psychology* (pp. 9–26). London: Sage.

Smith, J. A., Flowers, P., & Osborn, M. (1997). Interpretative phenomenological analysis and the psychology of health and illness. In L. Yardley (Ed.), Material discourses in health and illness (pp. 68–91). London: Routledge.

Smith, J. K., & Deemer, D. K. (2000). The problem of criteria in the age of relativism. In N. K. Denzin & Y. S. Lincoln (Eds.), *Handbook of qualitative research* (2nd ed., pp. 877–896). Thousand Oaks, CA: Sage.

Smith, L., Pope, C., & Botha, J. (2005). Patients' help-seeking experiences and delay in cancer presentation: A qualitative synthesis. *Lancet, 366*, 825–831.

Sparkes, A. C. (2001). Myth 94: Qualitative health researchers will agree about validity. *Qualitative Health Research, 11*(4), 538–552.

St. Denis, V. (2004). Community-based participatory research: Aspects of the concept relevant for practice. In W. K. Carrol (Ed.), *Critical strategies for social research* (pp. 292–301). Toronto: Canadian Scholars Press Inc.

Steckler, A., McLeroy, K. R., Goodman, R. M., Bird, S. T., & McCormick, L. (1992). Toward integrating qualitative and quantitative methods: An introduction. *Health Education Quarterly, 19*(1), 1-8.

Stephenson, J. M., Imrie, J., & Sutton, S. R. (2000). Rigorous trials of sexual behaviour intervention in STD/HIV prevention: What can we learn from them? *AIDS, 14*(Suppl 3), S115–S124.

Strauss, A., & Corbin, J. (1990). *Basis of qualitative research: Grounded theory procedures and techniques.* Newbury Park, CA: Sage.

Strauss, A., & Corbin, J. (1998). *Basics of qualitative research: Techniques and procedures for developing grounded theory* (2nd ed.). Thousand Oaks, CA: Sage.

Sundell, K., & Vinnerljung, B. (2004). Outcomes of family group conferencing in Sweden. A three year follow up. *Child Abuse and Neglect, 28,* 267–286.

Sword, W., Jack, S. M., Niccols, A., Milligan, K., Henderson, J., & Thabane, L. (2009). Integrated programs for women with substance use issues and their children: A qualitative meta-synthesis of processes and outcomes. *Harm Reduction Journal, 6*(32), 1–17. doi:10.1186/1477-7517-6-32.

Tashakkori, A., & Teddlie, C. (2003). *Handbook of mixed methods in the social and behavioral sciences.* Thousand Oaks, CA: Sage.

Temple, B., & Young, A. (2004). Qualitative research and translation dilemmas. *Qualitative Research, 4*(2), 161–178.

Tesch, R. (1990). *Qualitative research: Analysis types and software tools.* Bristol, PA: Farlmer.

Thomas, J., Harden, A., Oakley, A., Oliver, S., Sutcliffe, K., Rees, R., ... Kavanagh, J. (2004). Integrating qualitative research with trials in systematic reviews. *BMJ, 328*(7446), 1010–1012.

Thompson, C., McCaughan, D., Cullum, N., Sheldon, T. A., & Raynor, P. (2004). Increasing the visibility of coding decisions in team-based qualitative research in nursing. *International Journal of Nursing Studies, 41*(1), 15–20.

Thorne, S. (2006). *Can qualitative meta-synthesis make a contribution to evidence-based practice? Issues and challenges in an era of research integration.* Panel presentation for Advances in Qualitative Methods, Academy Health, Seattle, Washington.

Thorne, S., Jensen, L., Kearney, M. H., Noblit, G., & Sandelowski, M. (2004). Reflections on the methodological and ideological agenda in qualitative meta-synthesis. *Quality Health Research, 14,* 1342–1365.

Thorne, S., & Paterson, B. (1998). Shifting images of chronic illness. *Image: Journal of Nursing Scholarship, 30*(2), 173–178.

Thorne, S., Paterson, B., Acorn, S., Canam, C., Joachim, G., & Jillings, C. (2002). Chronic illness experience: Insights from a metastudy. *Qualitative Health Research, 12*(4), 437–452.

Tobin, G. A., & Begley, C. M. (2004). Methodological rigour within a qualitative framework. *Journal of Advanced Nursing, 48*(4), 388–396.

Tracy, S. J. (2010). Qualitative quality: Eight "Big-Tent" criteria for excellent qualitative research. *Qualitative Inquiry, 16,* 837–851.

Treloar, C., & Rhodes, T. (2009). The lived experience of hepatitis C and its treatment among injecting drug users: Qualitative synthesis. *Quality Health Research, 19*(9), 1321–1334.

Tugwell, P., Robinson, V., Grimshaw, J., & Santesso, N. (2006). Systematic reviews and knowledge translation. *Bulletin World Health Organanization*, *84*(8), 643–651.

Tukey, J. (1962). The future of data analysis. *Annals of Mathematical Statistics*, *33*(1), 1–67.

Turner, H., Boruch, R., Petrosino, A., Lavenberg, L., de Moya, D., & Rothstein, R. (2003). Populating an international web-based randomized trials register in the social, behavioral, criminological, and education sciences. *The ANNALS of the American Academy of Political and Social Science, 589*, 203–223.

Valadez, J., & Bamberger, M. (1994). *Monitoring and evaluating social programs in developing countries: A handbook for policymakers, managers, and researchers.* EDI Development Studies. Washington, D.C.: The World Bank.

Voils, C. I., Hasselblad, V., Crandell, J. L., Chang, Y., Lee, E., & Sandelowski, M. (2009). A Bayesian method for the synthesis of evidence from qualitative and quantitative reports: An example from the literature on antiretroviral medication adherence. *Journal of Health Services Research Policy, 14*, 226–233.

Waddell, C., Lavis, J. N., Abelson, J., Lomas, J., Shepherd, C. A., Bird-Gayson, T., . . . Offord, D. R. (2005). Research use in children's mental health policy in Canada: Maintaining vigilance amid ambiguity. *Social Science and Medicine, 61*, 1649–1657.

Wade, C. A., Turner, H. M., Rothstein, H. R., & Lavenberg, J. (2006). Information retrieval and the role of the information specialist in producing high-quality systematic reviews in the social, behavioral, and education sciences. *Evidence & Policy: A Journal of Research, Debate and Practice, 2*, 89–108.

Wadsworth, M. J. (1998). Designing a qualitative study. In L. Bickman & D. Rog (Eds.), *Handbook of applied social research methods* (pp. 69–100). Thousand Oaks, CA: Sage.

Walsh, D., & Downe, S. (2005). Meta-synthesis method for qualitative research: A literature review. *Journal of Advanced Nursing, 50*(2), 204–211.

Walters, L. A., Wilczynski, N. L., & Haynes, R. B. (2006). Hedges team. Developing optimal search strategies for retrieving clinically relevant qualitative studies in EMBASE. *Qualitative Health Research, 16*(1), 162–168.

Waterman, H. (1998). Embracing ambiguities and valuing ourselves: Issues of validity in action research. *Journal of Advanced Nursing, 28*(1), 101–105.

Weed, M. (2005). Meta interpretation: A method for the interpretive synthesis of qualitative research. *Forum: Qualitative Social Research. 6*(1). Retrieved from http://www.qualitative-research.net/index.php/fqs/article/viewArticle/508/1096.

Weed, M. (2008). A potential method for the interpretive synthesis of qualitative research: Issues in the development of meta-interpretation. *International Journal of Social Research Methodology, 11*(1), 13–28.

Weeks, L. C., & Strudsholm, T. (2008). A scoping review of research on complementary and alternative medicine (CAM) and the mass media: looking back, moving forward. *BMC Complementary Alternative Medicine*, *8*(43). DOI: 10.1186/1472-6882-8-43.

Whittemore R., Chase, S. K., & Mandle, C. L. (2001). Validity in qualitative research. *Qualitative Health Research*, *11*(4), 522–537.

Wikberg A., & Bondas, T. (2010). A patient perspective in research on intercultural caring in maternity care: A meta-ethnography. *International Journal of Qualitative Studies in Health and Well-being*, *8*(5). doi: 10.3402/qhw. v5i1.4648.

Wilczynski, N. L., & Haynes, R. B. (2002). Robustness of empirical search strategies for clinical content in MEDLINE. *Proceedings of AMIA Symposium*, *1*, 904–908). D020001793.

Wilczynski, N. L., Marks, S., & Haynes, R. B. (2007). Search strategies for identifying qualitative studies in CINAHL. *Qualitative Health Research*, *17*(5), 705–710.

Wilson, K., & Amir, Z. (2008). Cancer and disability benefits: A synthesis of qualitative findings on advice and support. *Psycho-Oncology*, *17*, 421–429.

Wong, S. S. L., Wilczynski, N. L., & Haynes, R. B. (2004). Developing optimal search strategies for detecting clinically relevant qualitative studies in Medline. *Medinfo*, *107*(Pt 1), 311–316.

Index

CPSIA information can be obtained
at www.ICGtesting.com
Printed in the USA
LVOW01s1441010216

473175LV00021B/1007/P